1500 Limericks is dedicated to no one in particular

But if you smile or laugh that much the better

Copyright

My Newfoundland-Labrador friend Freddy,
his balance is unsteady.
He grins and asks. "Is dinner ready?"
I look around with total regret.
And say, "Not yet."
I apologise to Freddy.
--
"Fred, your bedroom is a mess.
Look how awful you dress.
My feet are blistered and I have cramps in my legs.
I was so nervous to see you that I spilled a carton of eggs.
I was under extreme strain and duress."
--
There's a knock on the door and the telephone is ringing.
At the same time the kitchen oven is dinging.
Two burgers in the oven are almost done.
The cook book I used isn't the right one.
The burgers tasted a bit stinging.
--

I hate to admit it when I make a mistake.
But one day I set the oven on Broil instead of Bake.
And there were more discomforts ahead.
Sometimes I wish I remained in bed.
I have had it with baking. That is all I can take.

--

Fred asks, "Aren't you finished cooking dinner yet?"
I get insulted, you bet.
I reach for the kitchen knife.
He loses an earlobe although I wanted his life.
Fred is the strangest person I ever met.

--

Don't get me wrong. I love the city of Victoria.
And the scavenger hunt was a lot of fun with Gloria.
But if I live until next year.
You won't find me here.
As I will be moving to Astoria.

--

I thought I could love no other.
Until I met your brother.
Love may be beautiful. Love may be blissed.
But I only slept with you because I wanted to be kissed.
Please don't tell my mother.
--
Of loving beauty you float with grace.
If only you could hide your face.
Then I could love your smile and eyes.
But darn it, you are good at telling lies.
My time with you has been a disgrace.
--
The beauty of love.
Is a heavenly dove.
From the sky above.
That gives a loving couple a shove.
As thereof.
--
Pretty Janet is my size.
To her mother she often lies.
What she has been taught at school.
But she's no fool.
To tell mother what books she reads or buys.
--

My darling. My possible wife.
Marrying you would screw up my life.
Although you say that are you are kind,
loving and hot.
This describes everything you are not.
Living with you would be a life of strife.
--
I see your face when I'm dreaming.
That is why I always wake up screaming.
What inspires this amours rhyme?
Two parts vodka and one part lime.
This limerick has no meaning.
--
Jenifer was hot to trot.
Her affection many sought.
Till the cute buttercup.
Got knocked up.
Before a wedding dress she bought.
--
When the Pastor addressed Jim and said,
"You may now kiss the bride."
Jim was nervous and about to hide.
Because Jim's and Julie's lips could not meet.
With Julie's high heels at her feet.
She stood towering over her groom and cried.
--

Once a choir boy, Justin turned to romance.
And fell in love with Margarita at first glance.
In public view.
And in bed too.
Both showed the world how to give peace a chance.
--

A bottle of wine, a poetry book and like Jack Horner.
Linda and I discussed our marriage in our bedroom corner.
We discussed forgiveness, finances and pain.
credit card debts, misbehaving kids and the constant rain.
And not to be a mourner.
--

When things go wrong, and sometimes they will.
My search for a lasting mate was uphill.
When my funds were getting low and debts high.
I wanted to smile but had to cry.
So I kept taking a Vicks Nyquil.
--

My marriage is difficult to figure out.
From the beginning it was a bout.
I however, was determined to fight when hardest hit.
And my parents urged me not to quit.
Otherwise it would have been a rout.
--
Finding a wife has its twists and turns.
And as one is searching for a mate learns.
Not to give up though the pace may seem slow.
But then you may have a rejection and another blow.
And find your heart filled with scars and burns.
--
Canadian singles find new ways to meet.
Now they can tweet.
On line.
Which is fine.
If Devine gives one a treat.
--
When Rebecca Malone.
Was in the Arctic zone.
On the iPhone.
I didn't feel lonesome.
At home alone.

The iPhone I bought yesterday.
Is an old model, quite passé.
I found that it needs a case.
And had been thrown of base.
In the end I had to throw it away.
--
There are many uses for the iPhone.
Including to text when I'm alone.
As a camera, and a wakeup alarm.
To email and in the event someone is committing harm.
I'm happy with the iPhone I now own.
--
Following a hiccup.
Tom and Anne purchased a garbage pickup.
Then went bankrupt.
Had a marriage breakup.
In the end there was no makeup.
--
Sam Fix.
And Sandy Dix.
Along with several hicks.
Entered politics.
Despite their tricks – nothing ticks.
--

Teddy.
Get ready.
To go steady.
With Heady.
She's ready, already.

--

Oh you beautiful one!
Whose heart I have just won.
You are a man that is loveable and kind.
However, with your strange behind.
You are unable to run and have fun.

--

While taking a walk, snowflakes were falling.
Winter traffic was crawling.
Snow birds were calling.
Coyotes were pet mauling.
While oil prices were falling.

--

A year ago.
I was with Joe.
It was 30 below.
As Joe is elderly and slow.
Nowhere did we go.

--

Neighbor Michael.
Says: "It's time to Reduce, Reuse and Recycle.
Canadians are among the most prolific garbage producers on Earth.
Take it for what's it worth.
Asians are the most prolific who use a motorcycle.
--
The best Canadian joke I ever told.
Was when I was 19 years old.
My career was about to unfold.
When my lemon car I sold.
At a time when I was very cold, foolish and bold.
--
In Canada razor blade sales are dropping.
It appears there's no stopping.
Instead of shaving, men are growing a beard.
Which to some their face appears weird.
And wives are furious and hopping.
--

In an Olds, Alberta convenience store Abbot was annoyed and began swearing.
At a customer request, so uncaring.
And said, "Young lady you are the dregs,"
And she replied, "No, I don't have frog legs.
It's the 5 inch high heels I'm wearing."
--
Cyber bullying is on the increase.
Young men want teenage girls to hug and squeeze
On the internet they also invite them to have sex.
That's what happened to Ruth Becks.
Who now suffers a suicidal disease.
--
Canadian Dean.
And Swedish Irene.
After being divorced for five years are getting married again.
They won't say when.
Except that their vows will take place before a pastor and a well-known queen.
--

In Ghost Town, Saskatchewan, farmer Anthrope.
Had a poor wheat crop.
The selling price did drop.
So he had to stop.
And now he's growing beer hop.
--
Officials hope to.
Contain an outbreak of the Avian flu.
In the B., C, Fraser Valley poultry farms.
As the virus is causing harms.
And authorities don't know what to do.
--
In Hamilton, teenager Bunny.
Was funny.
When he wanted to become a drummer in a rock n roll band.
And said, "The best in the land.
And make loads of money."
--
In Dryden, Ontario when Roy.
Was a baby boy.
Before he went to sleep his mother used to sing a lullaby.
So that he wouldn`t cry.
But his sleep enjoy.
--

In depressed Windsor, Ontario 30-year-old Fraser was a dude.
Because of the recession he was in a bad mood.
He couldn't find a job.
So he began to rob.
Because he had no money for food.
--
A secret to save your marriage.
Even if it isn't your heritage.
Rebuilt your trust.
Or the marriage will bust.
Even if you drive a golden carriage.
--
How to get over your marriage past?
Is not to be too fast.
To get your spouse to change.
Within a certain time range.
Otherwise your marriage will not last.
--
Hilda is a divorcee.
Which everyone can see.
Hilda and her husband did not agree.
That at 65 he should be a retiree.
Once they were divorced the husband said, "Whoopee!"
--

Recently a married couple rented a cottage near Lake Superior.
Once they were in the interior.
They each looked into a mirror.
The husband however, felt inferior.
Because of his unusual derriere.

--

Two young people were walking on a Toronto street and appeared unhappy.
Mildred said to Pappy.
If you want me to be happy.
Stop being crappy.
And so snappy."

--

For better quality of life.
Is best to be married to a trusting wife.
Don't live on a wing of prayer.
As there are no results there.
And your life will become full of strife.

--

Sandy Hart died of a broken heart.
As she wasn't very smart.
Her husband Bart left her for another woman.
Who was more human.
And had a better living chart.

--

For Peter Wong.
It's wrong to sing a filthy song.
After a hand shake.
I'll make him a cake.
And then, I`m gone.

--

Xylitol is an artificial sweetener.
For him or her.
While it is safe for humans it's dangerous for hogs
And dogs.
But not if you're a Sir.

--

Canadian oil prices drop.
When will it stop?
A short while ago the price was on top.
So when did the price pop?
For the answer contact oil analyst Fiddly Bop.

--

Ah. Ah. Ah!
Canada.
From the Pacific, Arctic to the Atlantic.
Because oil prices are dropping, there is panic,
At the moment there nothing more to say except, Ha. Ha. Ha."

--

Canadians are talking.
About foreign workers who are working.
Without a work permit.
And most admit it.
During tough times they are squawking.
--
Go where I go.
Then you will know,
Night or day.
That is the way.
To review your bio.
--
Poppy, Hoppy and Snappy.
Poppy is floppy.
Hoppy is scrappy.
Snappy is unhappy.
Mixed together they are crappy.
--
I don't know why the budgie bird sings
When the doorbell rings.
Or Kitty cat leaps.
The floor mother sweeps.
Or the joy to mother the budgie brings.
--

Anthony Huff.
Is hot stuff.
He went to a casino.
In Reno.
And wins plenty in Blind Man's Bluff.
--
Occasionally, when I`m lonesome and blue.
With nothing in particular to do.
At the foot of my bed.
I stand on my head.
And wonder what is new?
--
I`ll get the information in a minute of two.
Because I enjoy doing things for you.
I`m at your beckon call.
But dog on it all.
Sometime there are things that I cannot do.
--
I`m not certain about my next verse.
As a method to converse.
But it's clear to me.
From what I can see.
In a dictionary, that is how words are disbursed.
--

Rubba, dub, dub.
Lord, thank you for the grub.
There is hunger and no meat.
And if there is meat,
It tastes like mud.
--
Lord, thank you for those who are able.
To enjoy the food found on this table.
Bless the spaghetti and the jam.
The toast, eggs and the ham.
And bless the cook, Alice Grable.
--
Lord, bless mother for the coffee she makes.
Which gives us belly aches.
We give you thanks. We give you praise.
That mother has better days.
When she makes the milkshakes.
--
Awake, the day has turned to a night!
Not the moon or the stars are in sight.
The air in the stillness is dry.
And I wonder why?
During the month of June, Canada geese are still on their northern flight.
--

When I heard children with a mournful cry.
And an open eye.
"Mother, please shut the door.
Or else we'll not see Kitty cat anymore!"
At the time Kitty was chasing a mouse and I kept wondering, why?

--

Genealogy is one of my desires.
To complete our family tree before my father retires.
Where he was borne, no one knows.
Searching is an experience with several unexpected blows.
I must have the family tree completed before his life expires.

--

As a genealogist don't send me a set of new dishes.
Because I have certain wishes.
I don't need a new kind of a game.
All I need is the family name.
That is one of my wishes.

--

A new tape recorder would be great.
To record an ancestor's birth date.
And the beginning of her life.
That had become my father's wife.
And a lifetime mate.
--

My heart doesn't yearn for a ring.
What I want is a cheaper thing.
That would put a diamond into shame.
Instead send me Mary's surname.
And the happiness it would bring.
--

To have my heart beating with joy.
Bring me a genealogist toy.
Don't bring me a suitcase.
Only a family name with both a date and a place.
And if you were born, a girl or a boy.
--

The Saskatchewan gopher says to my sister Rose.
"You have a funny-looking nose."
The rodent has little time to stay.
And after the comment, runs away.
With a bushy tail and sore toes.
--

Desmond Brown lives on a Vancouver lot.
Whose cabin was about to rot.
The yard had soil of clay.
Where he planted a vegetable garden, each May.
And the grass on the lawn turned to pot.
--
Desmond Brown had to leave his lot.
Because his annual taxes he paid not.
Was it because Desmond was ill?
After each day he took a Tylenol pill?
"No." he said, "I have dementia and forgot."
--
The night wind cries its soft and endless theme.
Then in the dark I have my nightly dream.
That the stars and the moon are in flight.
The stars to the left. The moon to the right.
What a delight! What a dream!
--
At 4:00 a. m. as the rooster crew.
My fright grew and grew.
A scavenger was found in the garbage tank.
Who identified himself only as Hank.
In Edmonton finding a street person in a garbage bin isn't new.
--

A potato peeling has no taste.
And was thrown in a garbage bin as waste.
"Don't do that", said a cook.
"The peeling is nutritious, take a look.
You threw the peeling away in haste."
--

In Saskatchewan, Andy Handy did not carouse.
In a divorce he lost his house.
For better or worse he was out of line.
As his marriage he could not define.
And thus, Andy lost a loving spouse.
--

In the British Columbia town of Ladysmith,
Judith Griffith was out of shape.
Her head looked like an oversized grape.
Bearing arthritis on her shoulder.
As she got older and older.
Her life style began to agape.
--

In Sexsmith, Alberta, the truth about Harry.
Is a bit scary.
As he wants to marry.
A ferry.
By the name Bing Cherry.
--

In Delisle, Saskatchewan every rose has its thorn.
Once in a while a child is born.
During a snow or electrical storm.
After one blows a horn.
From midnight until mid-morn.
--
In Roblin, Manitoba, Suzann Daze.
Is in a state of amaze.
Every 2 days.
She visits the Greys.
A family of well-known gays.
--
In Kenora, Ontario, Paula has a new man.
With a tan from Japan.
He's a birdy.
That is 30 and flirty.
His language used is sometimes dirty.
--
In Beauharmois, Quebec, Jocelyn Whig.
Is hooked up with Marcel who is big.
She went to a beauty salon to buy him a wig.
When she came back he was doing a jig.
Which Jocelyn did not dig.
--

In Edmundston, New Brunswick, it's a fact.
Jenifer St. Marie was doing a juggling act.
In doing so, she was getting thin.
After dating Jim Flynn.
A foreign worker who had a one-year contract.
--

In Digby, Nova Scotia, Kim's marriage to Clarence Dover.
After 2 months was over.
After an ugly fight.
In the middle of a Saturday night.
Both declined to talk in over.
--

In Montague, PEI on line Esther Devine.
Says she's fine.
Except some say she looks like Michael Jackson.
And says, "Sorry. I have no reaction.
Until I enjoy a glass of wine."
--

In Happy Valley, Newfoundland-Labrador.
Lucy Tyler.
Is a perpetual smiler.
One day while jogging.
It began fogging,
With luck Lucy became a compiler and a computer firm hired her.
--
When I was in Newfoundland-Labrador.
I met Wendell Orr.
A 50-year old labourer.
Near the Atlantic shore.
With whom I had chatted once before.
--
In the Nunavut city of Iqaluit an aboriginal mother says, "Here the kids grow up fast.
And last.
Our Lola is seven.
Arthur is eleven.
Thank goodness their early childhood is past.
--

In Nunavut snow drifts are rooftop high.
Children can't go to school, stay home and cry.
There's load of snow
And the temperature is 50 below.
Residents wonder: "Why so cold. Why oh why?"

--

While in Nunavut I had an encounter with three polar bears.
And I developed frightful scares.
After staring at me for an hour and I had no rifle, they turned around and moved towards the Arctic Sea.
That is when I realized the bears were hungry.
And thankful the bears were giving me only dares.

--

In the Canadian Banff National Park, a grizzly bear was hunting near the trees.
Where he ran into a hive of honey bees.
Along came another bear to the hive.
And soon there were five.
A most interesting sight one ever sees.

--

In the Northwest Territories town of Fort Smith, Ellen met her match.
While with Allan she was playing snowball catch.
It was a fairy tale moment.
And as there was no apparent opponent.
Soon there will be a baby to hatch.
--

In Whitehorse, Yukon, a prospective bride was asked, "If you have someone sing at your wedding, which it would be?"
"For me, it probably would be Michael Buble or Beyoncé."
"And what about the wedding dance?"
It would be similar to the cancan in France.
Which I would want you to come and see."
--

A good mechanic is difficult to find.
AMA is looking for you if you are talented and kind.
To help members who are in trouble.
Even if the vehicle engine only has a bubble.
To help vehicles of any kind.

--

While in Australia.
With Dahlia.
We saw an alligator and a kangaroo.
An Australian owl that kept asking, "Who? Who are you?"
And I spoke to an Aboriginal lady by the name of Ophelia.
--

In Emerson, Manitoba there was a musician with a flute.
When another musician damaged his uniform suit.
But he played throughout the night.
Till the other musician took a Winnipeg flight.
And avoided a lawsuit.
--

Let the wise debate with me.
The state of the universe let it be.
Some say the world is coming to an end.
I say, ``Nonsense there are thing we can amend.
Let`s be brothers and sisters and say to each other, ``I love thee".
--

In the city of Saint Clair, Michigan there was a realtor name Claire.
Who had a magnificent pair.
This is what she thought.
Until she got caught.
In the vendor's underwear.

--

In the town of Fort McLeod, Alberta, Pretty Amorous Sue.
Had a date she knew.
However, the coroner had found.
The couple had drowned.
While on Waterton Lake paddling a canoe.

--

At the Newfound-Labrador community of L'Anse aux Loup.
There is a poet named Gaytan Capture who enjoys her pea soup.
And writing limericks that are clean.
And not obscene.
She writes with a stoop.

--

I'm not certain about my next verse.
As a method of how to converse.
And it's clear to me.
From what I can see.
That is how words disburse.

In Glace Bay, Nova Scotia, an elderly realtor originally from the Isle of Skye.
Reckoned, "Old realtors never die.
Though without any doubt.
When their heartbeat runs out.
There sales will not be high."
--

A real estate salesman in Saskatoon.
Never learned to eat with a spoon.
He would fork up his soup.
With a bending stoop.
Too bad he died so soon.
--

In the New Brunswick city of Moncton, there is gentleman named Fred.
Who said as he climbed out of bed.
"There is no heaven I am sure.
But I have to endure.
The alternative when I'm found dead."
--

In my lifetime I had made mistakes.
Sometimes those are the breaks.
I got married and joined the crowd.
This made my parents proud.
For the good sense that it makes.
--

In Lac due Bonnet, Manitoba, there was a salesman named Joe.
Who had lost his get up and go.
Without thinking.
He began drinking.
And eventually found his sales were slow.
--
Occasionally when I'm blue.
With nothing in particular to do.
I stand on my head.
At the foot of my bed.
This isn't a lie, it's true.
--
My pet dog Fido can hardly see.
One day I took him for a walk with me.
When I felt something warm.
I looked down with alarm
Fido thought my leg was a tree.
--
When things go wrong as they sometimes will.
My search for a lasting wife was uphill.
I however, was determined to fight back when hardest hit.
As my parents urged me not to quit.
I never did keep still.
--

My search for finding a mate had its twists and turns.
As everyone sometimes learns.
Not to give up though the pace may seem slow.
But then I received another rejection I didn't know where to go.
Leaving my heart with scars and burns.
--
Often I was frustrated and nearly gave up.
When I thought I had captured a victor's cup.
However, another rejection came down.
As I imagined my bride wearing a wedding gown.
And was prettier than my pet pup.
--
At last my search for a mate came to an end during a starry night.
We were married and she became my Mrs. Right.
Because I had learned to fight back when hardest hit.
And things were rough but I did not quit.
While going through the emotions of anger, depression, rejection and fright.
--

Heather Brown never knew.
When she bought her high heel shoe.
What she had to do.
When she found a missing screw.
And then on a cue went for a brew.
--
Who is the richest woman in the world? –
Holly Branson is the daughter of famous billionaire, Sir Richard Branson.
Who has a daughter but no son.
Holly has a medical degree and involved in her father's business activity.
Including the African Nativity.
Holly is reported to have twins soon one of which could be a son.
--
Harry and Kelly.
Each had a large belly.
And went to an Industrial park.
Where there was lot of pollution and it was dark.
After an hour they came home kind of smelly.
--

While drinking and dating,
Irene and Sam soon began mating.
They were joyful of mind.
Gentle and kind.
And often went skating.
--

While in the Philippine city of Cebu.
Two Canadians were new.
After enjoying a San Miguel brew.
They each decided to have a tattoo.
A day later he went to the zoo where they caught the flu.
--

I expect whatever you say is true.
No matter if your eyes are brown or blue.
The man with you.
I knew.
Who had difficulty with his brew.
--

Whatever is wrong with you?
Hurts me too.
I've been waiting to date you.
But I guess one with Britany will do.
Until I find someone new.
--

I saw a shooting star and thought of you.
And figured my troubles were through.
Until I had a better view of you.
My passion grew and grew until you had said.
"To converse positively, there's too much to do."
--
I promised you.
Once I had a better view.
Now I felt what you had said wasn't true.
So I went out with Hugh.
And it's "Farewell" to my ex and to you too.
--
Jane, I hope you are feeling better.
Now that I gave you a woolen sweater.
To tell you the truth I rather eat spring rolls.
Than wearing a sweater with holes.
Or become a debtor.
--
In a Mallaig, Alberta restaurant, Rosetta
cooks meal with spices.
That are delicious and the nicest.
Her menu is made with authority.
Enjoyed by Mallaig's majority.
And sold at low prices.
--

Upon my word. Upon my soul.
In the Saskatchewan town of Kamsack, Mary found a gopher hole.
It's not very deep.
Just large enough to have a sleep.
By a burrowing mole.
--
On Jessie Lake, Alberta, there are migrating birds and a frog.
That first sits on a lily pad and then on a log.
The frog cannot eat.
Anything that is sweet.
Because of the continuous fog.
--
In a way.
It's O. K.
To dine with my sister Kay.
During the month of May.
And not to have a bad day.
--
The lips you press.
After I say, "Yes."
Sets my heart a flutter.
While I'm enjoying a sandwich with peanut butter.
With my mother no less.
--

On Lac Ste. Anne in Alberta, there were two lovers in a canoe.
One was Muslim and the other a Jew.
One held a paddle.
And the other a rattle.
What they were discussing I do not know. Do you?
--
At age 15 a young lady in Edmonton.
Was out to have a lot of fun.
She would ring a neighbor's door bell.
And then ran like hell.
Eventually she became a nun.
--
Ralph.
Lives in the Ontario city of Guelph.
Where he has wealth
But poor health.
Because he wasn't taking care of himself.
--
Aba.
Babba.
Plays at a Victoria Inn.
His Stradivarius violin.
Once done he enjoys a java.
--

Mary.
Is always contrary.
If it should be milkshake with a strawberry?
Listen to a canary
Or date Harry?
--

In Sherbrooke, Quebec, on his death bed.
The ill Pasture said:
"Bring me a Revenue Canada tax man and a lawyer.
When they came the lawyer.
Asked: "Why the 2 of us? And was told:
"Jesus died between 2 thieves and that is the way I do not want to go when I'm dead."
--

When I was in Yorkton, Saskatchewan, a stranger asked me. "Can you borrow me ten bucks?"
I asked him why he needed the money? He replied. "I want to go hunting for ducks."
I replied, "A shucks.
Your request sucks.
As my money presently is in a state of flux."
--

In Saskatchewan town of Hudson Bay.
Barefoot Bob is debonair.
Dresses with utmost care.
Not one hair out of place.
And not a whisker on his face.
When he goes out for a bit of fresh air.
--
I have seen or heard them all.
The Big Ben. Vatican, China's wall.
The Niagara River rapids fall.
And Canada geese call.
Each spring and fall.
--
Dick was holidaying in Edmonton.
To see West Edmonton Mall and have fun.
Then he went to Seba Beach and have some sun.
But he forgot his sunscreen while on a run.
Dick's sunburn wasn't fun by the time his day activities were done.
--
Danny wanted to go on a trip.
All the way to the moon in his home-made spaceship.
The ship sputtered and did roar.
As it began to soar.
It exploded and so ended Danny's moon trip.
--

In vibrant Gravelbourg, Saskatchewan there are gophers on each street.
With long tails and skinny feet.
One can find gophers in a café and convince store
There are gophers everywhere and more.
That look charming and oh, so sweet.
--
H is for Head. Shoulders, Knees and Toes.
Eyes. Ears. Mouth and Nose.
I'd love to be Hippopotamus that can swim and dive
And dance the jive while still alive.
That's the way my life goes.
--
In Morris, Manitoba, Sam has an aging problem.
That he can't solve it and them
When he reached 50 and became older
He grew wider and shorter
Leaving him in a state of conundrum.
--

In Dauphin, Manitoba, Tony Onod
End joys eating food that isn't odd.
What he enjoys the most.
Is ham eggs and toast.
Next on list that someday he can enjoy a dish of fish cod.
--
In Kapuskasing, Ontario, Ted.
Keeps a bird on his head.
And hardly spoke.
Because a short time ago he had stroke.
After he enjoyed a coke.
--
My wife Faye is on the phone again.
And again,
My mood is getting sour.
As this time she's on the phone longer than an hour.
This time talking to a friend in Afghanistan.
--
In past years.
I enjoyed many bottles of beers.
And now my wife says strange things about me that she hears.
That derives her to tears.
And all sorts of fears.
--

This is my birthday. A special day.
Everything should go my way.
The sun should shine, The birds should sing.
My friend on the phone will ring.
To see if I have gray hair and how often do I pray.
--
Stan.
An electronic engineer in Japan.
Can't understand
Why his wife Anne.
Doesn't love him but an electronic repairman.
--
In the Alberta city of Wainwright.
Walking the streets after midnight.
In the moonlight.
Is a wonderful sight
One is safe and no need of a possible fright.
--
Joey with no ruffle
Took a shuttle.
To visit Venus and Mars.
The 9 planets and distant stars.
When Joey returned to Planet Earth, he said the trip was enjoyable.
--

In Princeton, B. C. Ken enjoys his salami and slices it with a knife
And had the strangest experience in his entire life,
When he asked his wife, "Kiss me."
She said, "I will but it's not for free."
For the rest of his life Ken led a sad life.
--
In Telkwa, B, C., Shirley Jones.
Enjoys her vegies but not the chicken bones.
She rather eat a steak instead.
Often scratches her head.
And a dietician she phones.
--
When our refrigerator is cleaned out.
Children run about.
And shout.
"Where is the Brussel sprout?"
The children are hungry. There's no doubt.
--
I hear my wife.
Sandy gripe.
The tomatoes, what will do with then when they become ripe?"
I do want to change the quality of my life.
Should I cut down the pants with a knife?"
--

At a gathering, despite a small commotion.
There was lot of emotion.
When the elephant blew her trunk.
The sound woke up a dozing skunk.
One could smell the spray all the way to the Pacific Ocean.
--
At a party the elephant said, "I have been handed a note.
It's from the owl which the bird wrote.
And confirmed by a sheep.
That it's past midnight and time to go home and sleep.
And that is OK because most of us by now have a sore throat."
--
Hearing the goose and duck protest, a parrot began to cuss.
"Oh dear, don't cuss," cried out an octopus.
A baboon emailed a message that he was in an air balloon in Saskatoon.
And an elk and a moose said they were planning a trip to the moon.
The elephant wondered why all the fuss?
--

At a party the elephant MC told all the animals to be at ease.
Poodle Doodle couldn't be at ease because he was always chasing fleas.
An almost extinct whooping crane said wild animals, birds and fish without a measure.
Are Canada's everlasting treasure.
"Don't make them extinct. Please".
--
In Saint Paul, Alberta, Lizzie Gordon who like in Tall River, Massachusetts, Lizzie Bordon.
Had taken an axe and gave her mother 40 whacks.
When this was done.
She gave her father another 41.
According to the judge the homicides weren't committed for pleasure or spite.
But because her parents couldn't find work and were returning to Jordan.
--

In the Alberta town of Vegreville, while at the Farmer's market to buy vegetables and fruit.
Paul Hill met vegetarian Agnes Calorie, wearing a swim suit.
Agnes suggested that Ed should not eat meat but beans instead.
Only beans and no meat Paul thought could cause a climate change as he would have to fart and scratch his head.
And wherever he would go, he would have to be careful not to go, "proot-proot."
--
Ed stopped at a drugstore in the Alberta town of Elk Point.
Where a clerk asked him if he wanted by a medical marijuana joint.
Since Ed suffered from arthritis.
And the clerk, bronchitis,
Ed was delighted because the drugstore was a checkpoint.
--

In the Alberta town of Glendon, Slava
Kalinsky had a beard larger than Karl Marx.
He loved to go fishing and play darts.
His beard was so large that small birds had a nest in.
The local preacher said that Mr. Kalinsky had committed a sin.
When he had tossed the tiny birds to the sharks.
--

Near the city of Brandon, lives Evelyn Tonne
whose garden herbs are tender and green.
Good enough to eat by a king and a queen.
Today the garden is weed-free.
A year ago embarrassing to see.
A patch of earth that once was the most unsightly ever seen.
--

Sometimes my face turns red.
To recall how Ted's head had bled.
As his Honda was making a left hand turn on Main Street.
He was broadsided by a Toyota driver friend he was to meet.
He never did because of the two vehicle accident, Ted was dead.
--

In the Yukon community of Beaver Creek.
Tom and Joe felt weak.
So they decided to dine.
And enjoy Tom's home-made wine.
They drank even when they felt weak and meek.

--

Ira was paddling a canoe on the Fraser River.
It was cloudy, cold and he began to shiver.
Suddenly Ira was thirsty and wanted to have a drink.
And met another canoer by the name of Sam Brink.
Who was an alcoholic and couldn't deliver because he had trouble with his liver.

--

In a Regina debate there were ayes and noes.
And when there is controversy that is the way it goes.
Some members wanted a skyscraper built that almost reached the sky.
While others disagreed and wanted to know, why?
Not to regret the project they chose.

--

At the Alberta Bonny Lodge while baking, the dough had to be knead.
And flavoured with sesame seed.
And to Mrs. Brennan the baker wrote.
"Please read the recipe and take note."
Unfortunately Mrs. Brennan was illiterate and couldn't write or read.

--

This I know: Where there is darkness, there is also light.
Whether during the day or at night.
Dear mother, I want to take a minute from you.
To thank you for everything for me you do.
Without being engaged in a worldly fight.

--

I nearly died from laughter each time I read a Joe Remesz book.
Example: How on one day his wife while in Prince Rupert deep sea caught 2 fish on the same hook.
"Fun and Laughter" should be mandatory reading for.
Very sports minded daughter and son.
No matter if they are honest or a crook.

--

In the distant Saskatchewan village of Oops.
Dan Price always snoops.
If his neighbor uses an axe.
And if he has paid his property tax.
Finding out, Price then goes and poops.
--
In the Ontario city of London, Jane often goes to a garage sale,
Accompanied by Richard, a male.
At a great discount they buy many articles of their wishes.
Including, utensils, clothing and used dishes.
One day they even bought a three- inch nail and an old scale.
--
In Mississauga, Ontario as a Mayor, 86-yer old Hazel McCallion, has stepped down.
Hazel was a successful mayoralty candidate in 12 municipal elections of the town.
Re-elected 10 other times.
For a woman these were difficult times.
The 'Hurricane' however, is delighted she still has an interest in women's hockey and to have worn a municipal crown.
--

Reuben Ayuban wasn't joking.
That he wanted to quit smoking.
Two packets a day.
Now no pay.
His heart needed stroking.
--

Josh had a daily routine of enjoying a Coke.
Relax under a California oak.
And have a tobacco smoke.
At a time that he was broke.
His habit he couldn't revoke.
--

After midnight while sleeping, Mike awoke.
And found his condo full of smoke.
Windows were broke.
He began to choke.
So did the other folk.
--

Douzo Dobri is a 50 -year-odd Toronto beggar.
A ham and egger.
Who is homeless and has nothing of value.
Nothing he tries to sell you.
Until he meets with Gordon McGregor.
--

Jose Valentino has an addiction for gambling.
One day while rambling.
At a Reno.
Casino.
He met a Filipino who noticed that Valentino was undergoing a chemo and a
at the s slot machine had a side effect and was trembling.

--

Mark, my brother-in-law,
Had trouble with a zoning bylaw.
He wanted to build a liquor store
But city council said: "Sorry, No more."
In the end Mark had to hire a lawyer–in-law.

--

A worm is an insect that makes us silk.
A cow is an animal that gives us milk,
Beef, butter, cream and a milkshake
Which is easy to enjoy and to take.
No matter what is your ilk.

--

A stranger in tattered clothing.
Was watching a Markham, Ontario musician as a piano stool he was unloading.
The stranger then offered 50 bucks but the musician shook his head.
 And said:
"Sorry, I'll need the antique stool to do my piano composing."
 --

What percentage of Alberta Strathcona County isn't arable?
That means the land is unusable because it's terrible.
Statistics show.
That on the land one is unable to grow,
Because each spring there is still three feet of snow.
And the weather often is unbearable.

--

In the Alberta town of Bonnyville a young man was wearing a Pontiac hockey cap.
Excited, after purchasing a computer he sat on his mother's lap.
His mother was admiring the computer, scanner and the printer.
When a day later, her son approached her as a sprinter.
And unequivocally said: "This computer is a piece of (s)crap".

--

There was a faith healer in Bonnyville.
Who said: "Although the pain isn't real.
When I sit on a pin,
It punctures my skin.
Now you know how I feel."

--

Albert Greshner lives near Grande Prairie
With 2 children and his wife Nelda Mary.
Each winter when the weather is nice.
They go fishing to the nearest lake ice.
Seldom they catch any fish, but on their way home see a lot of mice.

--

In the Alberta town of Valleyview.
To farmer Dan, I once knew.
The weatherman had said: "Please don't cry.
You can trust me and plant vegetables
because the weather will be dry."
But in the end, because of a draught there was
some dew but the vegies were only a few.
--

Elderly Sam's newspaper obituary read:
"Sam Elder of Saint Albert at 93 is now
dead."
During the month of February.
Sam rushed to the cemetery.
To discover that because of a printing error
this Sam wasn't dead because he still sleeps in
his bed.
--

A Wainwright, Alberta Military Furniture
Store says – "The more you buy, the less you
pay.
Use our website – www Furniture Store.ca.
Buy one mattress and the second is free.
We have a 50 percent discount if you are a
retiree.
The specials take place only during the month
of May.
--

If you live in an apartment, you go through a weekly vicious cycle.
Taking care of your garbage and to recycle.
Dispose discarded food that has no taste.
And has become a kitchen waste.
Everyone has to do it even in the Alberta town of Saint Michael.
--
Mistake money makes while buying a house.
For me and my spouse.
Is that the first word money has learned is to say is," Good Bye."
As I was short for a mortgage payment and it made me sigh.
My spouse was disappointed and I ended up in a doghouse.
--
My favourite internet search engines are Google and Yahoo.
Just between me and you and my friend Nap too.
In Israel the engines are used by Prime Minister Benjamin Netanyahu.
And chairman of the United Nations Ban Ki-moon, uses the same engines too.
And after they find their sought information they each yell, "Wahoo."

In the Manitoba town of Carman, there are 2 kinds of suburbanites. Those who are rich like Mr. Lee.
And those who use to be rich like Mr. Kennedy.
Mr. Lee got rich because he was involved in a fraudulent mortgage scam.
And Mr. Kennedy became poor because in his store he did not sell enough jam.
Both did what they wanted to do when their time was free.
--
Mary Anne. Marry Anne.
Better get married as quickly as you can.
You are now forty and about to go through menopause.
Without help from Santa Claus.
You'll never get married to a loveable man.
--

Vancouver City council has suggested that the next city hall should be built out of glass.
And taxpayers would be delighted and smile when they pass.
One would never have to worry about rain or snow.
Or the north wind blow.
There was concern however, if taxpayers didn't like the structure, they would throw
Rocks at it en masse.
--

In the New Brunswick city of Bathurst, Henry Clark was suffering from a bout.
With a handicap Henry suffered from tremendous gout,
Which suddenly it went on the attack.
On all his body joints including those in his back,
Henry was suffering a lot of pain, there is no doubt.
--

In the Alberta town of Vermillion, lived a civilian by the name Arthur Fillion.
Whose yearly income was one-million.
He was a CEO of many companies throughout the world.
And his vision was never blurred.
His next move is to stash his cash until his yearly income becomes one-billion.
--
Last week.
Ned in Alberta's Pincher Creek.
The blowing wind was so strong that it was difficult to strive.
And stay alive.
Because Ned did not wind protection seek.
--
Following a double bicycle spill, Jerry and Jane went up a hill and at the British Columbia Coast.
And purchased a condominium where at one time lived a ghost.
They enjoyed watching the sea, the hardwood floor.
And also the security door.
They enjoyed the unpolluted air the most.
--

There was a ghost in a Lunenburg, Nova Scotia home.
Who each night decided to roam.
It bumped and banged.
It hummed and sang,
And wouldn't leave the proprietor alone.

--

In the Prince Edward Island town of Souris, there was a skeleton in a tomb.
Who invited a spirit to share his room.
They spent the whole night.
In a vicious fight.
Over which should be more frightened by whom.

--

As Matt was walking near the city of Medicine Hat he came upon a grass snake.
Earlier in a Snake Book Matt had read under such circumstances to remain calm and not to disturb a snake when it's awake.
The book also said to stand still, look up at the sky.
And then the snake straight into its eye.
Matt didn`t know what next steps to take.

--

In the Alberta town of Beaumont, Alec Goodyear had ringing in his ear.
That he would become deaf was his greatest fear.
Doctor Greene diagnosed the number of rings was twenty-four.
That's 10 more than he had before.
When his ear was really, really sore.

--

Two tourists arrived in the British Columbia town of Pouce Coupe.
And at a hotel where they found a room to stay,
One said the correct pronunciation of the town was Poos Coupe, the stress on Poos
And the second said the stress was on Coupe (ay or ee)
At any rate, whichever pronunciation you choose to be right, because of the oil and gas, the Peace Country, it's an excellent community to make hay.

--

Calgary is fast becoming a cosmopolitan city with new buildings going up almost instantly.
Mind you, sometimes incoherently.
I recently passed by the Chinook Motel,
And then the Skyline Hotel.
When I asked Mayor Naheed Nenshi about the buildings, he replied, "They
were built fast and extravagantly."
--
While driving on Alberta's Highway 16,
Frank and Bill didn't drive far.
 And stopped at a Mundare town bar.
Where each enjoyed a garlic sausage and glass of gin.
And then threw the empty bottle into a garbage bin.
When a preacher wanders in and says, "You guys are committing an environmental sin.
Because you are living like a czar."
--
Listen again and come close.
And I'll show you a T-shirt my mother sews.
The colors are white, yellow and green.
Or a color in between.
It depends on which direction the window blows.
--

In the Ontario city of Barrie, I did not see a canary but met Jerry, a peevish schoolboy.
Who gave his parents pain and joy.
It was a whimsical relationship.
At times more difficult than flying a spaceship.
A relationship of pure love the parents did not want to destroy.
--
During a forest fire in British Columbia as I can tell.
There was more smoke than in hell.
The fire was the largest in 100 years.
Driving residents out of their homes into tears.
What else? No one in Kelowna is feeling well.
--

In the Newfoundland-Labrador town of Corner Brook, 2 middle aged men were debating the charms of a beauty.
One admired her face, hair and lips and described her as cutie.
The second then said. "Take away her smile, blue eyes and figure and what you got?"
The first then scratched his head and said, "She reminds me of my wife who is hot."
The beauty was a snooty and her name was Janice Flutie.

--

In the Alberta community of Rife.
Andre Fife was in search of a wife.
First he drove the prospect in different cars.
And then took her to liquor bars.
Despite the efforts Andre remained single all his life.

--

In Neepawa, Manitoba there was a rascal named Random.
In the end the judge said, "Instead of being beheaded. Random.
I'm having you wedded."
Now Random
And his wife live in tandem.

--

In Regina there was a villain named Brand,
Who RCMP says had died by his brother's hand.
He dogged insistence.
On ending his existence.
He succeeded, but not as planned.
--
In the Yukon city of Dawson there once was a gold miner named Eric.
Whose arguments were spheric.
He always wanted to see a golden crown.
And never let down.
As his arguments were a bit esoteric.
--
There once was a hunter in Whitehorse, Yukon named Julian.
Dark haired and with eyes of cenulean.
From head to heal.
His body looked as if it was made out of steel.
His ass however, was by no means clean.
--

In the Yukon town of Haines Junction, Al Benedict faced a bear attack.
And lost his arm after the bear gave him a whack.
A neighbor planned,
To give Al a hand.
But later, Al wanted his arm back.
--
In the Saskatchewan town of Arborfeld.
Tom Brown fell in love with Agnes Sheld.
While driving Tom's car Agnes hit his horse.
Which led to a sudden divorce.
After Tom was trying the car damage to weld.
--
Shelly.
Lives in an Alberta town of Coutts-Sweetgrass chalet.
One day she crossed the Canadian-American border to see a ballet.
With friends Sandra and Kelly.
 When they returned home. Both had an aching belly.
--

In Yellowknife there's miner named Charlie Hays.
Where Pastor Raptor gives him a lot of praise.
However, they aren't discreet.
And each Sunday when they meet.
The Pastor always asks how much money in the collection basket, Hays pays.
--
In Hay River NWT there was once a sailor named Cane.
Who proposed his own death to feign.
Then, "Brothers," he said.
"I'm not really dead."
So somebody killed him again.
--
A Hay River, NWT young girl by the name of Dar,
Her father bought her a car.
No fun did she derive.
Because she had no license to drive.
Before developing any driving skills, Dar did not drive far.
--

In Inuvik, NWT there was a taxi driver named Abby.
Who drove his cabby.
For 30 years.
In that time he had seen passengers with laughter, fears and tears.
is constant driving made his life flabby.
--
In Norman Wells, NWT to order a pizza a wild goose was accompanied by a wise fox.
The each put on their warm socks.
While near the McKenzie River.
 They began to shiver. A pizza they did not deliver.
And sat on the nearby pile of large rocks.
--
In the NWT community of Fort Laird, I sat near Matilda to enjoy a cup of tea.
Just as I feared it would be.
She had a rumbling abdominal.
Which was phenomenal.
And those present thought it was me.
--

In Fort Smith, NWT an auto mechanic named Hank.
Because of the cold weather he had to start his car with a crank.
After several explicit words and a whack.
Hank injured his back.
And said: To push the old car is like pushing a military tank."

--

A pansy in Khartoum,
 Took a lesbian to his room.
They argued all night.
Over who had the right.
To do what and to whom.

--

A wealthy connoisseur.
In the district of Big Sur.
Lived in house that had siding made out of cedar instead of fir.
Following an investigation to make sure
That the siding was placed by the contractor in error.

--

Near the Alberta hamlet of Anshaw, one day.
Farmer Art Shaw was cutting his hay,
When the mower broke down.
For a repair he took it to town.
This seems to happen during each month of May.
--

In the Alberta hamlet of Ardmore.
Lived Igor Fillmore.
Who to the waitress said, "Here's a deuce.
For a glass of orange juice."
Once I drink it, I'll feel fine forever more."
--

The prefabricated house Dan lives in is small.
It has a portable kitchen and a wall.
Dan used FedEx to move it from Calgary to Cold Lake.
Where for a meal he preferred fish instead of a steak.
Dan is 7 feet tall.
--

While the Edmonton the Police Chief was speaking,
In his office, the floor was creaking.
He spoke about the service police can provide.
And a traffic victim who had just died.
For which more information he was seeking.
--
In the B. C. village of Slocan.
Lived a despondent man.
Who was in love with Maryanne.
He owned a gun, fired several shots and then ran.
RCMP is searching to find him as quickly as they can.
--
There was a forest fire near the Manitoba village of Snare.
Flames, smoke and an awful smell were in the air everywhere.
As an alcoholic fugitive was passing by.
He did not shed a tear or cry.
Because he was overtaken by the alcohol and did not care.
--

In Penticton, British Columbia the wine you drink. The lip you press.
And the way you always say, "Yes."
 Makes my heart beat with joy.
The method you employ,
To mark our true love, no less.
--
In Vancouver the water flows under the Lions Gate Bridge.
It's a method of drainage.
Out flows the sewage and debris,
Thrown into the Fraser River by the likes of you and me.
The river filth then flows in into the Pacific Ocean including the rotten cabbage.
--
In Vancouver it was raining and the streets were like pools.
Drivers were driving too fast and became fools.
They soaked their brakes.
 And made many mistakes.
'Because they didn't have the right tools.
--

In Winnipeg an elderly pedestrian was knocked over.
By a visitor driving a Rover,
And said: "I know the street code.
And rules of the road.
Unfortunately I wasn't wearing my lucky charm, the 5 leaf clover."

--

"Life is just a moment that belongs to you." said Stu.
"If you are happy or blue.
Live your life. Live it now.
Your guardian angel will show you how.
Because when you die, you can't take anything with you."

--

In the Nunavut community of Taloyoak (formerly known as Spence Bay) the seal pudding I loved so long.
Wasn't eaten when something went wrong.
I ordered a ginger ale in a cup.
When my stomach went burp;, burp, was upset and went up and up.
The pudding was eaten after I sang a Twiddle-Dee - Dwindle Dum song.

--

Ah, love! You shall not conspire.
When my heart is on fire.
If you do, my heart will be shattered to bits.
And even worse, if it splits.
I won't be able to sing with the church choir.
--
I love my grandson.
Except when he leaves my car headlights on.
And when this is done,
He eats my favourite chocolate bun.
And says his behaviour is just for fun.
--
The Manitoba sun shifts into the night.
While at the Winnipeg Airport I'm waiting for my flight.
For 3 hours I wait and wait in vain.
 So I took a train.
And reached my destination on time, all right.
--
As soon as the Alberta Slave Lake Hockey star died.
Those in Doms Gastropub having a beer, cried.
Ted Spring had played in the NHL for fifteen years.
And as one hears.
He had no secrets to hide

David married my sister Rose.
Where they live, no one knows.
But still the gemstone ruby kindles in the vine
Which is mine.
And you can see it even if it snows.
--
Come, fill the cup with wine. It is spring.
And time for another fling.
Our 25th wedding anniversary takes place in June,
And it will come not too soon,
To have the church bell ring.
--
Yesterday.
I did say,
"The month is May.
And time to harvest the hay.
Even, if it's my birthday."
--
In the Alberta town of High Level.
For Mike Bevel,
Alzheimer's strikes early.
His demeanor becomes squirrely,
Squirrely, but not like that of the devil.
--

During a heat wave in Alberta, a power plant was shut down.
Putting a strain on the electrical users in town.
Citizens were urged to reduce their power use.
Because a shortage of the grid juice.
And those who did, did it with a frown.
--
Ah! Fill the glass with wine.
A second time.
It's worth to repeat.
As I can still stand on my feet.
With help of the Divine.
--
Taking care of our parents can be a difficult task.
That is why they seldom ask.
But we want the best for them,
And do not condemn.
Even if the request is made when a parent is wearing a mask.
--

On the kitchen shelf one can find our house key.
Used only by my wife and me.
It opens the front and back door.
And more.
It is also used to the bathroom when we want to go and pee.
--
In Canada the climate is warming and climatologists are crying.
They say we get closer to frying.
But one year it's hot.
The next year it's not.
Sometimes I think climatologists are lying.
--
UN scientists say: Florida, Bangladesh and Vietnam soon will not exist.
And with a warning persist.
And there will be a high tide in 3 places
The entire regions destruction faces.
And soon will be added to the 'Good Bye' list.
--

Nature is alive on channel 9.
Which is a good sign.
When birds hit a power line.
Electrical power is disrupted and EPCORE a new line did design.
The best of its kind.
--

Can one compare global warming skeptics to Galileo (1564-1642).
The father of modern science and better known in Italy as Leo.
Galileo met opposition for believing the Earth moved around the Sun by the Catholic Church and spent the rest of his life under house arrest.
Today we recognize that the church was wrong and Galileo had past his theory test.
And Planet Earth spins around the sun, even in Tokyo.
--

Environment Canada has issued a nation-wide weather warning.
From coast to coast to coast the weather will be storming.
There will be lot of snow, freezing rain, and the temperature may reach 50 below
So don't go to work, stay at home and if driving, go slow.
For an updated weather forecast, check you news media in the morning.
--
The changing world with a digital tool.
Meant for bright people and not a fool.
Where a happy hour.
Can suddenly go sour.
And one can jump into a swimming pool.
--
Sid.
Is in charge of the Toronto electrical power grid.
That carries energy to communities that make a bid.
Even if the communities are a distance away and famous for its squid.
And the contract price may be hid.
--

U. S. President Obama and the climate change make nature sing.
The president knows almost everything.
He says the proposed Canadian XL pipeline from Alberta to Texas is a wrong thing.
But accepted by Republicans and its right wing.
If not approved soon the rejection to the Canadian oil industry will be a major sting.
--
Juliet and Eliot were holding hands.
While viewing the Alberta oil sands.
It was during a summer breeze
That each other their hand they did squeeze.
After vising the tar sands, they viewed the community uplands.
--
In the Alberta town of Panoka when it came time for Mel Sanoka to find a mate.
He began to search for a date.
God made Adam and Eve.
But not Adam and Steve.
Common sense made Mel to go straight.
--

8-teen- year old Moe asked his friend Joe, "In the past year, you have been to which Alberta lake?"
Joe replied: "I have been to Sylvan Lake, Smokey Lake, Sandy Lake.
 Saddle Lake, Jesse Lake, Moose Lake, Flat Lake. Cooking Lake,
 Rat Lake, Wolfe Lake, Meadow Lake, Bear Trap Lake and Frog Lake.
But the lake I enjoyed most of all is, Cold Lake."
--
In the Alberta town of Devon.
When spring arrives, citizens believe they are in heaven.
Young girls are arrayed.
In best fashion displayed.
As soon as they are eleven.
--
World News Report –
Germany wins World FIFA soccer award.
Scotland to have an Independence election vote and is looking forward.
EBOLA outbreak in Liberia.
Gold discovered in Siberia.
Russia's Putin using his sword.
--

After watching television.
Ben Hoy in Miramchi, New Brunswick had a vision.
That a young boy he knew,
Had the flu.
That it was in a remission.
--
During the dusk of day.
To the Alberta city of Lloydminster I was on my way.
When suddenly my car went out of control.
After I had I hit a pesky pothole.
All I could do is pray.
--
In the Manitoba town The Pas, a poet writes a poem about Ma and Pa, and having writ.
About love and wit.
On every second line.
He would have a rhyme.
Then review every word of it.
--
God the earth did make.
And then followed the snake.
He gave us other animals and birds.
Some which are kind of absurd.
And He also gave us forgiveness to give and to take.

At the city of Toronto, the Entertainment stage at Massey Hall, above and below.
A magician was putting on a show.
Tricks of illusions and sleight of hand to view.
That weren't new.
As people would come and go.
--

In the Saskatchewan town of Fort Qu'Appelle with a vision and a prayer.
Mel said to a homeless child, "We'll get you there."
With the child he built a relationship and a future.
As the child grew Mel did nurture.
For the young man to operate an Esso service station, healthy, and strong with a lot of hair.
--

As I drove on Highway 16, near the Alberta town of Spruce Grove, I came upon garbage that had been thrown.
Near a canola field that had been sown.
The garbage consisted of beer and pop cans, all kinds of paper,
Plastic bags, old rags and a paint scraper.
Who dumped the garbage is still unknown.
--

Another depression think some.
Foreclosures will come.
It could be another crash.
People without cash.
And wonder where their next paycheque will come from.
--
I gaze at the stars.
The moon and Mars.
They are all so bright.
On a clear winter night.
Even after I spend time in the city liquor bars.
--
Ford will be the first to open a branch on Jupiter and Mars.
To market its UVs, trucks and cars.
McDonalds will be the first to open a fast food restaurant on the moon
That will be open from midnight until noon.
This could happen during the month of June under bright stars.
--

When I lived in a Doha, Qatar.
I learned how to play a guitar.
Between me and you.
I also learned how to play a piccolo and a kazoo.
I played the instruments for those who lived near and far.
--
In between my dazzling career, I lived in Poland.
Syria and Nigeria and Iceland.
I also lived in Thailand and Nepal.
But the country I enjoyed living in best of all.
Is when I lived in Holland.
--
When I was in a hotel in Lima, Peru.
There was a 7,1 earthquake and after I had nothing to do.
The hotel rumbled and shook.
I couldn't read my book and chef could not cook.
In Peru earthquakes are nothing new.
--

My Hotel friend, Pat Kelly.
Has a potbelly.
Whenever he has a beer.
It is dangerous to come near.
For fear his fat will turn into a jelly.
--

In the Alberta community of Fort Kent.
My nose was a bit bent.
As there was lot of snow.
And I had nowhere to go.
I decided a video game to rent.
--

Ed, a young motorcyclist in Fort Kent.
Had a serious accident.
At the Bonnyville junction.
His brake stopped to function.
Having no funds left, Ed spent the night in a tent.
--

Ed lived in Alberta's village of Fort Kent.
But couldn't pay his rent.
So he bought a tent.
And wherever he went.
Received a compliment.
--

There was a lady in Fort Kent.
Who was known for her unusual prank.
When a friend came to visit her, she would pull out a skunk.
From her trunk.
That stank.

--

There was an elderly lady in Alberta's Fort Kent
Who slept on a bed made of cement.
The bed was well used.
And parts of her body were bruised.
On the back of her head she had a dent.

--

While traveling to Bonnyville, Faye found herself with a flat.
Throughout she kept asking, "What is that?"
Eventually she found that her spare,
Wasn't there.
Just some empty bottles and an old mat.

--

Don't drink if you are going to drive.
If you do, you or a pedestrian may not survive.
You do not drive any quicker.
If you drink liquor.
It's best to stay alive.

Traveling broadens your mind.
Together the new sights you will find.
It's more fun.
If you are traveling with someone.
No matter who, as long as they aren't blind.
--
When you travel a lot.
To places that are cold or hot.
One day my wife says, "Please.
Give me a squeeze.
Because where we were, I forgot."
--
On Planet Earth there is no one like you.
What I'm saying is true.
When making my stew.
And when I have the flu.
You are the greatest friend I ever knew.
--
Your lovely smile I like.
Under a spotlight or while taking a hike.
You remind me of a peach..
When your lips I try to reach.
At a time when I'm on strike.
--

One thing you should know.
In Canada there is lot of snow.
It can be very cold at night
Although the snow is white.
The red poinsettias in a hothouse seem to grow.
--
I'm a world traveler and have visited –
Columbia, Bolivia, Costa Rica, Poland
Argentina, Mexico Iraq, Holland
Tunisia, Papa New Guinea, Australia
Brazil, Panama. Wake Island, Malaysia
Easter Island, New Caledonia, Iceland
--
Ecuador, Haiti, Trinidad, Belarus, Algeria
Belgium. France, Czech Republic, Bulgaria
Ukraine, Bermuda, Wake Island
Austria, Germany, Russia, Thailand.
Croatia, Philippines .Cyprus, Tunisia
--
Canary Islands, Denmark, Estonia, Finland
Portugal, Spain, Norway, Switzerland
Botswana, Ethiopia, Ghana, U. K
Turkey, Sweden, Latvia, U. S. A.
Ireland, Japan, China Nigeria, Scotland
--

The most corrupt countries I visited are --
Somalia, Philippines, Syria
Venezuela, Hatti, Libya, Eritrea.
Chad, South Sudan, Afghanistan
North Korea, Yemen, Uzbekistan
Iraq, Cambodia, Guinea Bissau, Nigeria
--
When Joseph Knuble first climbed the famous Swiss Matterhorn Mountain he was 15 years old.
The Matterhorn is more than 4000 meters in height and while on the top one can get cold.
In 1865 the first accent took place was by English physicist Edward Whymper.
However, it wasn't during winter.
But during the month of July we are told.
--

Nigeria's Boko Haram is staging cross-border attacks and recruitment.
It's an extreme, violent militant, terrorist Islamic movement.
That thus far has killed more than 5000 civilians, abducted more than 500 women and children.
Including kidnapping 276 school girls where Western education is forbidden.
The world no longer should stay silent and take retaliatory action at the earliest moment.
--
Romanians like their new president Klaus Johanis.
Because the former mayor knows his biz.
Its 25 years ending a Communist rule.
And children now are able to go to school
With a new democratic government, that the way it is.
--
Dan,
A handyman.
Strong and untiring,
And now retiring.
As quickly as he can
--

In Bellville. Ontario, James Guy
Is a wise guy.
Who had his first taste of a turkey.
That was a bit murky.
He enjoyed eating turkey meat but didn't know why.
--

In Sackville, New Brunswick, Sue Chu.
Was turning blue.
But on a cue she got himself a tattoo.
Between me and you.
Why? She still hasn't got a clue.
--

To his Selkirk, Manitoba friend, Ted and his friend sat in a car and said, what was true.
"My wife Betty told me we are through.
Because she says I'm too fat."
Ted's friend told me that.
"Well, you can't have your cake and Betty too."
--

In the British Columbia village of Alert Bay
there once was a tiny fish that could talk
And wanted to learn how to walk.
It got out of the sea,
And came to see me.
And apprehensively said, "Quick, before I get picked up by a hawk".

--

After having a drink of wine.
I decided to recline.
And headed for the refrigerator
Where popped up an alligator.
Tied up with a binder twine.

--

When I first met Simon Moor.
He was in drunken stupor, that's for sure.
He could not properly walk.
Or talk.
He was a person I could not endure.

--

Manitoba Scientist, Adam Dery.
Had an incomprehensible theory.
That was incomplete.
And also obsolete.
That made many scientists weary.

--

In British Columbia, during the month of March.
In the town of Langley, Nellie uses corn starch.
When baking her pies and cakes.
And anything else she bakes.
For a picnic under the Montessori Golden Arch.
--
There was a lady on the island Bahrain.
Who had an extraordinary brain.
She was tall and lean.
Her disposition was clean.
And she had the highest IQ ever seen.
--
There was a girl in the state of Montana by the name of Joanna.
Who wanted to live in Lethbridge, Canada.
So she had a banana, switched on her radio antenna, and did another thing.
When she slipped on her engagement ring.
And crossed the border with Canadian friend, Dominic Santana.
--

In the Manitoba town of Virden, 86 years old Baldy Cherry was a geezer.
He would only eat food that was in his freezer.
He first suffered from gout and then the flu.
In both instances he suffered until he was blue.
And consequently became a sneezer.
--
In the British Columbia town of Fort Saint John, Bobby Baun would go to a dance
And rock n roll with his 2 aunts.
Where each fought off a stinging bumble bee.
And then each said, "Look what is biting me!"
Because of the bee sting Bobby danced only until he peed his pants.
--
I walked into a Alberta town by the name of Canmore where at the liquor store.
I bought myself a bottle of brandy once more.
After I drank the entire bottle.
I was about to open my car throttle.
But boy oh boy, was my head ever sore.
--

A retired soldier in the Alberta town of Killam.
Lived Henry Fitzwilliam.
Who was repairing a military drum.
That was used during World War 1.
He wanted it to sound like: rap, rap, rap, bum, bum. bum.
--

In the Prince Edward Island city of Summerside, a veteran soldier was blind on one eye, And used a monocle on the other.
During wold war 11, he was helping General Douglas MacArthur.
Why did this happen is still a mystery but its certain.
When one unveils the museum curtain,
Whatever the soldier historically did, he also loved his father and mother.
--

In Canada 40,000 people use medical marijuana.
That includes Bret and his sister Joanna.
They enjoy smoking pot.
Even when the weather is terribly cold or hot.
Their health however, improved not.
--

In the Alberta city of Red Deer.
Ivor Swear.
Would rhyme the letter D with me.
The letter C with HIV.
Ivor was an old-timer who at times has difficulty to hear.

--

In your life, which do you prefer the most?
Andy says "Sex is dandy".
Mandy says, "A chocolate candy."
Sandy, a vigilante, says, "I enjoy having sex, sucking a candy and drinking a brandy.
Later still, when I'm cranky, Viagra may come in handy and for a breakfast toast."

--

In Toronto a fly by night internet guru by the name of Shoru said, "Sam, if you have the money?
I can find you a honey.
Using internet software which with one magical button click.
From hundreds of resumes on the screen you can pick.
Pick mates that are pretty and chummy."

--

Sam thought the guru Shoru internet plan was a scam,
As soon as he discovered his computer was filled with spam,
And later the guru had said, 'It may seem too good to be true.
You may change your mind after you see the video I made especially for you."
About the guru's sales pitch, Sam did not give a damn.

--

At Edmonton's Churchill Square one can meet weird people.
Even near the No Name Universal Church steeple.
Where I had met Miss Melody and she asked me to go swimming naked with her in Pigeon Lake.
Neither to her request I did not take, nor to the next, when she asked me to sign a petition to make strip poker an Olympic event which had already been signed by several prominent people.

--

In the British Columbia town of Golden,
when an opportunity did arise.
Stan Holden opened his eyes.
And invested in the Sure Profit Group.
Which had money to spend, lend and poop.
Once done, stress gone, Stan was happy to see the company dividend rise.
--
In the British Columbia town of Kimberley,
Lee's blind date was pretty Tara Bell,
Who had more curves than dimples and a hot temper as well.
Tara had a fascination for different men but several she had refused to date because of their smell.
On which we will not dwell.
All we know is that she told them to, "Go to hell."
--
While on an elevator at Edmonton's City Centre Mall.
I met pretty Anita Hall.
She had an excellent disposition so I made her a proposition.
And without competition.
Although it\t was a bit late, I asked her for a date, that's all.

Clara Drake lives on an Alberta farm fronting Muriel Lake.
As I was hungry and she was still awake, I asked her if she can make…
She interrupted and asked, ``Make what?" so I say ``A pancake.``
Clara said she could and then I asked if she could cook up a steak, she candidly
Replied, "Who do you think I am, a fake, for goodness sake."

--

The West Coast wonders include, the city of Victoria, Vancouver and Horse Shoe Bay.
Anyway, if I had my way, I would also include Penticton, Kelowna and Cranbrook to stay.
Summer or winter. Business or pkay.
The best time to visit these wonders is during the month of September and May.

--

As Ken and his wife Jane were driving on the British Columbia Coquihalla Highway.
Ken said, "Since this isn't a freeway I'll drive my way."
And carefully drove from Hope north to Kamloops via Merritt.
Where they stopped for lunch and Ken, who loves animals, purchased a ferret
And Jane, who loves birds, a parrot.
Then they drove, a night and a day until they reached Saskatchewan town of Hudson Bay.
--
In the Alberta town of Lac la Biche, the story of the day.
Was while Austin went fishing, his wife's horse went astray.
A search was conducted until June.
The horse was eventually found underneath a shining moon.
Enjoying the new crop of hay.
--

An adventure in the Alberta town of Brooks.
Is first to have a meal that Chef Bob Nooks, cooks.
And then attend the annual Medieval Faire which includes:
A "living village', ' dancing', and an 'artisan market'.
For an additional adventure contact the tour director, Michael Barcket.
This done, you will have a better idea how the town of Brooks looks.
--
If you aren't in a hurry.
Then you should visit the vibrant community of Fort McMurray.
Where people from throughout the world come to work at crude oil with Syncrude and Suncore.
And more.
Also make certain to see the Oil Sands Discovery Centre as well as the UNESCO world heritage site of Wood Buffalo National Park where the animals can be dangerous but even if you are enjoying curry, are in a hurry, don't worry.
--

In Brandon, Donna wanted to see the Alberta Oil Sands.
At Fort McMurray she met engineer Seth who had soiled hands.
Although Donna was pretty.
And Seth's hands were dirty.
Both became flirty and shook hands.
--
In Fort McMurray there's a saloon
Where oil workers drink beer and croon.
Because of the oil boom.
Some even sing under the moon.
Praying the XL pipeline will be built soon.
--
When you visit the state of Alaska.
A tourist guide you can aska.
To view the majestic lakes and rivers, towering mountains, glaciers, and wild flowers.
That is an exciting part of the Alaska driving experience for hours and hours.
If you can't visit Alaska then try Alberta's Athabasca.
--

In Calgary, Alberta I'm a cattle herder.
I raise beef cattle and let me tell you further.
I own oil sands property near Fort McMurray.
And because of the pollution I'm not in a hurry.
To develop the open pit mine any further.

--

In British Columbia a suntan you are sure to get.
And when it rains you certainly will get wet.
You will love the West Coast.
Victoria and Vancouver the most.
British Columbia is a wonderful province, you bet.

--

In Saskatchewan just ask any farmer about the provinces recent success.
In the Western province that use to be in a mess.
The canola and wheat fields are blooming.
The oil, forest and potash industries do not need a grooming.
Saskatchewan during a process, you are a picture of a great success.

--

In Manitoba the winters are cold.
Each spring there always seems to be a flood, but the population is bold.
You have the Humanity Museum, a tiger at the zoo, Assiniboine and Red River.
And in Winnipeg a foreigner is most likely a miller.
Commencing in October, Manitoban's wishes the winter season is kept on hold.

--

Ontario you have memories of Canada defeating United States during the 1812 War.
And what's more.
You have the Great Lakes and Niagara Falls.
The Maple leafs in hockey and Blue Jays in baseball.
And that's not all.
Because of your prosperous position you at times leave other provinces a bit sore.

--

Quebec City is the capital of the province of Quebec.
Where to visit, one doesn't need to spend a large cheque.
Residents call themselves Quebecois and official language is French.
Where seldom if ever, one will find a stench.
In the province of Quebec one can visit the Museum of Civilization and not strain your neck.
--
William Warwick.
Lives in in the province of New Brunswick.
Which is bilingual (English-French) and a gateway to Atlantic Canada.
While enjoying banana.
One can visit Fredericton, Saint John, Moncton and the phenomenal Bay of Fundy, if you are quick.
--

One cannot help but feel the emotion.
The bonds Nova Scotians have with the Atlantic Ocean.
One can fish, and pick fruit in the Annapolis Valley.
In Halifax visit the famous Art Gallery.
And attend a bagpipe concert in Antigonish without a commotion.
--
Prince Edward Island is 1 of 3 Maritime provinces and is the smallest in population.
It has author Maude Montgomery and a Golf of Saint Lawrence location.
The backbone of the economy is farming on red sandstone and growing potatoes.
And a small amount of tomatoes.
Prince Edward Island and is capital Charlottetown, are an important historic part of the Canadian equation.
--

Whether you like to plan in advance or just go with the flow.
There are many things in Newfoundland-Labrador to see and go.
You can kayak with the whales in the morning and chase giant icebergs in the afternoon.
There are more varieties of English spoken in Newfoundland -Labrador than anywhere. else in the world that you will have to recognize the dialects soon.
It's difficult to understand the culture, especially if one is kind of slow.
An Arctic adventure awaits one in the territory of Nunavut.
While it's not on a regular route.
One can meet ingenious people and enjoy whale blubber in Iqaluit.
And in Igloolik, have taste of raw seal meat to eat. At Baker Lake.one can see a polar bear that is cute.
Just ask any Malamute. (Large Dog)
--

Northwest Territories is Canada's land of the midnight sun.
Where one can have a lot of fun.
Geological resources include: petroleum, diamonds, natural gas and gold
And we are told:
Participating in the Yellowknife Midnight Sun golf tournament, viewing the northern lights and to fish in Great Slave Lake will also provide an unforgettable experience for everyone.

--

In order to enjoy a pleasant journey one doesn't need a coupon.
In order visit Canada smallest territory – the Yukon.
One must stop at Whitehorse and Dawson City to recall the 1897 Klondike gold rush.
And where one still uses a sled dog to mush.
Once your exciting journey is completed you may want to rest on a Yukon futon.

--

The Yukon River flows into the Bering Sea.
On a boat with me was a pretty lady.
Who I tried to kiss.
But her lips I did miss.
And she said, ``You sir, can kiss everyone else but not me."

--

Saskatchewan has 16 cities including Lloydminster which traverses the provincial border with Alberta.
But not including Flin Flon which traverses with Manitoba.
Its population is in excess of 1.2 million. The province has the second fastest growing population.
Next to Alberta.

--

For a better Identity in Saskatchewan, Moose Jaw was nicknamed as Little Chicago and The Jaw.
Without a flaw Prince Albert is named PA.
And for Ma.
And Pa.
Regina is nicknamed Pile of Bones.
And Saskatoon, The City of Bridges where lawyer Merchant says,
"It's the law."

In Alberta Camrose is known as the Rose City.
Fort McMurray as Fort McMorderm,
Lethbridge as the Windy City.
Red Deer as Dear Rear and Edmonton as the City of Champions and Edmnchuck.
With luck.
Calgary was nicknamed as Cow Town and Grand Prairie, Swan City.
--

In British Columbia the city of Kelowna has been nicknamed as the Orchard City.
Trail as the Silver City.
Campbell River as the Salmon Capital of the World.
 Oliver as the Wine Capital of Canada and Abbotsford as the Berry Capital of the World.
Receiving the most publicity however, is Victoria known as the Newly Wed and Nearly Dead city.
--

Places nicknamed in Manitoba are: Brandon as the Wheat City.
Thompson as Hub of the North and Nickle City.
Winnipeg as Chicago of the North, The Peg, Wholesale City and Winterpeg.
Other communities haven't been nicknamed. What a pity.

--

Cities nicknamed in Ontario are: Ottawa as O-Town and Boy City.
Cambridge as Tri City, Hamilton as Steeltown. London as Forest City.
Oshawa, Canada's Motor City.
North Bay as The Bay. Sault Ste Marie as The Soo.
Waterloo as The Loo.
Toronto as Hog Town. Owen Sound, The Scenic City.

--

In the province of Quebec only 2 cities have been nicknamed.--
Montreal as Quebec's Metropolis City
Quebec City. City of Saints .and Sin City
And Sin City (a historical nicknames from the North American prohibition era)
And the biggest enemy wasn't Sarah.
But John Dillinger who was gunned down in Chicago in 1914 by a cop who to this day hasn't been publically named.

--

In New Brunswick the nicknamed cities are Fredericton, Freddy Beach,
 And Celestial City.
Saint John: Canada's Most Irish City. Fundy City and Loyalist City.
Moncton, The Hub City.
No other community was nicknamed as a city although they are pretty.

--

In Nova Scotia, the city of Antigonish is named The Nish.
And with their wish.
 Prince Edward Island, Charlottown has been nicknamed: Birth Place of Confederation.
In the other part of the nation.
In Newfoundland Labrador, Saint John's was nicknamed Newfiejohn John and Sin Jawn, where one can catch fish.
--
For your house roof replacement in the Alberta town of Morinville you need a roofer that one can trust.
Checking out his experience and credentials is a must.
Decide if replacement of the shingles is asphalt or metal
And the labour to be done is under warranty and if coincidental.
If you do not follow these instructions than your roofing project will be a bust.
--

Where on earth have you been?
I've been to countries where I haven't committed a sin.
Syria, Algeria, Spain.
Germany, Russia, Ukraine.
And Canada, the best county I have been in.
--
While on the sea.
Pretty Mable was with me.
We did agree.
To go on a spree.
With a Jaycee.
--
Where in Canada have you been?
And had not committed a sin?
I've been to Surry. Fort McMurray.
Vancouver and the town whose slogan is Don't You Worry.
And places too numerous to mention that I have been in.
--

In Alberta, where have you been?
That you did not sin?
I have been High Level, Harry Hill, Three Hills
Beaumont, Ardmore and Two Hills.
These are smaller communities I have been in.
--
While in Edmonton, what did you see?
Tell me:
I saw a duck and a goose.
A deer and a moose.
A Monarch butterfly and a yum, yum bumble bee.
--
What else did you see in Edmonton?
A moose that weighed more than a tonne.
Kingsway Mall.
City Hall.
Swarms of mosquitos and home invaders that were on the run.
--

In the small communities, what kept you busy?
Wondering where I can find Lizzie.
Cutting grass, looking for friends.
Chasing gophers and prairie hens.
All this made me kind of dizzy.
--
In your journeys, how did you travel?
With the use of a gavel.
By an airplane, train, a skidoo and a car.
But not far.
As many of the roads are made out of gravel.
--
And what animals and birds did you see?
Between you and me.
A crow chasing flies.
A parrot telling lies.
And Lucie the elephant making a pee.
--
In your travels, who were you with?
I was accompanied by Harry Smith.
Ed Remus.
And Danny Shemus.
That I was accompanied with Justin Bieber is a myth.
--

To confess your sins where would you like to go?
"If I did sin and had the dough.
I would like to be at a pilgrimage at:
The Shrine Anne de Beaupre in Quebec City, Canada, Medjugorje in Bosnia,
in Poland, the shrine of the Black Madonna,
Lourdes in France and in Portugal to pray at the Shrine of Our Lady of Fatima I would go, but slow.
--
Last July we took a trip throughout Alberta.
Me and, my globetrotting friend Roberta.
We visited Medicine Hat, Lethbridge, Calgary and Banff where we met Alberta's tour.
director Ed Stanff, who suggested we also visit Jasper, Edmonton, and Grande Prairie and someday visit Indonesia and Jakarta.
--

Last August we took a trip throughout British Columbia.
Where we canoed the river Columbia and in Victoria where we met with B. C.'s tour director Sam Secoria.
Who suggested we also visit Vancouver, the Okanagan and Prince Rupert and next year to tour South America including Brazil, Argentina, Peru and Columbia.
--
Last July we took a leisurely trip throughout Saskatchewan.
In our new Dodge Caravan.
And toured Regina where the RCMP does its training.
And then Saskatoon where we crossed many bridges, Prince Albert where we saw a prison and Yorkton where good things happen but it was raining.
The tour was a good experience no matter if one is a woman or a man.
--

We toured Manitoba during winter.
Where in Winnipeg, during a cold spell we met tour director W. C. Printer.
Who suggested we wear a buffalo coat and see a tiger at the zoo, fish for walleye in Lake Winnipeg and then have the time of our life by visiting other communities including:
Brandon where we watched the Wheat Kings play hockey and Beasejour.
Which was interesting that's for sure.
Evan if one is a summer sprinter.
--
A vacation on a Caribbean Sea Cruise
With excellent entertainment, food and booze.
Is ideal for one who is single.
An opportunity to mingle.
An experience one shouldn't lose.
--
In Kelowna, B. C, there's a skiing resort Big White.
Where one can have fun day and night.
A ski down the slopes.
Will rise up your hopes.
If you are sprite and your pocket book isn't tight.
--

While fishing in Prince Rupert on the sea.
A great fisherman Ed wanted to be.
Suddenly nearby a whale jumps up and roars.
Ed lost his two oars.
And his photo ID.
--
In the Philippines there`s a city named Cebu.
And a young lady I knew.
She picked her rice and placed it into a bucket.
When a caribao tried to drink from it.
She warned, `That you must not do."
--
In the Alberta Town of Cold Lake I found Filipina foreign contract worker Jessa, who was pretty and bright.
She was twenty and medium in height.
Jessa ate with bare hands, sometimes with a fork and spoon but never with a knife,
I thought she wouldn`t become my wife.
Because when she barbecued her lechcon she never gave me a bite.
--

There was a Philippine contract worker in Dubai.
Whose employer abused and made her cry.
One day she thought she would have some fun,
So she pulled out a gun.
After the damage was done.
She headed home to Manila and to her co-workers said, ``Goodbye, Dubai.''
--
In the Alberta community of Red Earth it was midnight.
The stars and the moon were bright.
Jose and Cresencio were deciding on a flight when they got into a fist fight.
Jose wanted to go to Spain and watch a bull fight.
Cresencio on the other hand wanted to go to the Philippines and watch a cock fight.
--

While in the Philippines.
I had seen:
Palawan and the volcano in Taal,
Pasajian Falls, Chocolate Hills in Bohol, and there, the nearly extinct tarsier monkey which is small.
The chaotic traffic in Manila is the worse I have ever seen.
--
For lifetime thrills.
One should visit the Philippine Bohol's 1500 rolling chocolate hills.
Boracay, Palawan, Iloilo, Mall of Asia with no frills or special skills.
One will find many thrills.
As Mother Nature your dream fulfills.
--
As the night wind cries its soft and endless theme.
I sit by my Philippine window absorbed in figuring out my dream.
From abroad each month, you send me a door-to-door balikbayan box.
That includes jewelry, canned goods, toiletries and socks.
The last box was the most interesting have ever seen.

I miss you my darling, and when I`m here in the Philippines, lonely and blue.
I always keep thinking of you.
When things go wrong as often they do.
I wish I was in abroad with you.
To prove that our love for each other is true.
--
There was an elderly man in the Philippines.
Who lived on rice and beans.
Much to his bliss.
His physician said this:
``Instead of the Philippines, why don`t you try living in the submarines?"
--
Philippine volcano Mayon has an eruption.
To be followed by lava explosion.
 Twelve-thousand people to evacuate.
And it better not be late.
In order not to have another historic disruption.
--
This is no laughing matter.
It was Philippines worst typhoon disaster.
When super hurricane Haiyan/Yolanda,
devastated portions of Asia.
Including Malaysia.
--

A sad day in the Philippine history chapter.Hurricane Haiyan/ Yolanda n barreled into the Philippines on November 8, 2013 striking the city of Tahloban.
Where many hearts were broken.
Killing at least 6,300 (and counting) and leaving 1.9 million homeless. The highest in Philippine history.
Which still is a world mystery.
And a Divine omen.

--

In the Philippine province of Mindanao.
Twelve piglets were born by a sow.
On the same day twin calves were born to a cow.
Everyone wondered how this could be, oh how?
While a puppy dog all he said was," Bow Wow."

--

In Filipino folklore an aswang is a vampire-like witch ghoul.
Well known and popular in Western Visayas as a night fool.
At night he transforms into as a cat, bat and most often as a dog.
With no dialogue.
The aswang enjoys harming children who aren't in bed or when not in school.
--
Philippines: An Asian nation.
Made up pf 7,107 islands and a 94- million population.
Despite the earthquakes, volcano eruptions, typhoon and mudslide calamities, without a reservation.
 Philippines, an excellent tourist destination.
It's a shame corrupt politicians have ruined its reputation.
--
In Edmonton there's Filipino doctor, Prudencio Perez.
Many patients he has.
There's Nap Comenelli,
Who has a problem with his big belly,
And the most interesting patient physician Perez has.

I often get phone calls from Filipino foreign contract workers,
Most of them aren't jerkers.
Although pretty Salome and Ligaya are flirters
Some are also liars and cursers.
But boy, oh boy, at fast food restaurants do the every make delicious burgers.

Each month Teofista, a foreign contract worker, sends a Balikayan box home to the Philippines.
Consisting of toiletries, electronics, clothing and designer jeans.
Often included are canned goods and candy for the girls and boys.
And a variety of toys.
This to each child brings a bundle of joys.
Like seldom ever seen.
--

The prominent religion in the Philippines is the 80-million Roman Catholic Church.
That one doesn't want to smurch.
Where contraception, abortion and divorce are illegal.
And the national bird is the eagle.
A prominent charismatic renewal group is El Shaddai headed by Brother Mike Vilarde with 5-million adherents throughout the world affiliated with the RC Church
--
In the Philippines Muslims are a minority.
Comprising 11 percent of a seniority.
Most Muslims live in the province of Mindanao.
Wondering how?
To have their own country with authority.
--

In the Philippines the Iglesia Ni Christi
(Church of Christ) was founded by Felix
Manalo in 1914.
He abandoned the Catholic Church while he
was a teen,
And claimed to be God's prophet.
Reasoning no one could stop it.
But he rejected the doctrine of the Trinity and
his new religion had elements of a cult which
many had never heard or seen.
--
Ferdinand Magellen (1480-1521) was a
Portuguese explorer.
During the Spanish colonization of the
Philippines to God unbeliever he said:
"Christianity is great, so why don't you come
over?"
Born in Portugal and served King Charles 1 of
Spain in search of a westward route to the
Spice Islands of Asia,
While in the Philippines Magellen and his
soldiers were in a state of amnesia.
During 1621 at age 42, Magellen was killed
by the ruler of Mancan Island, Lapu-Lapu,
Which many thought was a horror.
--

Lapu-Lapu was a ruler of Matcan, an island in the Visayas, Philippines.
He is known as the first native to have resisted colonization and conversion by any means.
Matcan is an island near Cebu and Bohol, And that's not all.
Lapu-Lapu is responsible for the death Magellen, it seems,.

--

Manuel Quezon (1878-1844) was the 2nd president of the Philippines;
And it seems.
Before that time the 700 islands were occupied by the U. S.
And Quezon fought for a speedy independence while under duress.
Which happened in 1935.A city was named after him. Quezon died in New York City with a conscience that was clean.

Philippine Papal Visits
- Pope Paul V1 was a target of an assassination in the Manila International Airport in 1970. The assassin, a Bolivian Surrealist named Benjamin Amor Flores, lunged towards the Pope with a Kris, but was subdued.

- Pope John Paul 11 visited the country twice, 1981 and 1995, The mass of the late pope in Manila (1995) was recorded to have been attended by 4-million people, the highest number ever recorded in papal history.
- Pope Benedict XV! Declined the invitation of Cardinal Gaudencio Rosales and CBCP president Angel Lagdameo to visit because of a hectic schedule.
- Pope Francis visited the Philippines during January 2015 and scheduled to visit again in 2016 for the 51st International Eucharistic Congress in Cebu.

On the TransCanada Highway near Regina, Johnny Hite.
Drove his sports car almost the speed of light.
The speed limit posted, he did not obey and that wasn't okay.
Johnny got caught by a traffic cop and then all he could do is, say, "I guess for the first time I'll have to pray".
--

In the British Columbia town of Revelstoke, Mr. Danny had a smoke and then hired an elderly nanny.
Whose first name was Fanny.
She had pigeon toes.
And Pinocchio's nose.
And because of her age was also called `Granny`.
--

In Winnipeg, drunken Investment consultant, Donald Fix.
Said he had all sorts of tricks.
"The quickest way to make money", he said.
"Is to raise bees and sell honey".
To be frank, the idea stank as liquor and bees don't mix.
--

In Winnipeg there's a fellow named Reg.
Who was caught kissing a neighbors wife by the hedge.
Along came his wife.
With a carving knife.
But nothing happened because Reg made a promise not to do it again with a pledge.
--

"Hi, Hi."
Sang a magpie.
"Ho, ho."
Sang a crow.
"Come and see us how low and high we can fly."

--

The seagull said, `This isn't a riddle.
And although I haven't got a fiddle.
I can sing a little."
And joined a frog sitting on a log, a sparrow on an arrow.
And together with other birds sang the song, Hi Diddle- Diddle.

--

The king of the animal world, the lion, with a wink.
Said, "I will now have a drink
With my friend, the mink."
A turtle said to the skunk:
"I'd drink with you too but you stink."

--

A loon looked towards the moon.
And then the racoon.
Together with a fork and a spoon.
Sang another tune.
This time accompanied by the baboon.

Dandelion, Dandelion, at one time you made me whine.
As I looked at the front lawn and your yellow obnoxious weed blossom did shine.
But now, no more, like before. You are useful for an upset stomach, intestinal gas, as a salad green, herbal tea and a root coffee, available at a health store.
And when I relax I also enjoy a glass of dandelion wine.

--

Mocking bird. Mocking bird.
You are the strangest long-tailed bird I ever heard.
You seem to sing a song.
That is sometimes wrong.
Because it's a bit blurred.

--

In the Alberta town of Manning.
Slim Canning.
Had a big chin.
After he drank his gin,
 He would ask, "What do you think of my fruit canning?"

--

When I stopped at the Winnipeg zoo.
I saw a monkey that looked like you.
It gave me a scare.
Because it had no hair.
So I didn't know what to do.

--

On the 630 CHED Sports News.
Brian Hall gives his daily views.
Why the Eskimos win.
And the Oilers lose.
And then says, "Win or lose I wouldn't like to be in their shoes."

--

There was a farmer near the Alberta Town of Smoky Lake that was attacked by a bear.
While he was still wearing his underwear.
And another farmer near Flat Lake, was attacked by a cougar, but.
Said, "I really don't care.
Because I was prepared and hit the cougar first with my rocking chair."

--

Near Thompson, Manitoba, Sammy Lim on a day that was dim, was exploring an old nickel mining cave.
And had a close shave.
When he stepped on a piece of sharp glass.
That ended up in his ass.
It was so painful that Sammy although brave, didn't know how to behave.
--
In the Saskatchewan municipality of Broadview, lived a muscular man by the name of Stu Wales.
Who I knew, and had strong teeth and the ability to chew nails.
It impressed friends he knew.
And me too.
And when finished, he didn't realize that his mouth ails.
--
In the British Columba town of Rossland.
Ray and Faye recently arrived from Holland.
And lived next to a babbling brook.
The rippling water they mistook
 For a music performance by a loud rock n roll band.
--

Roy and Mary LaValley is a couple I know that lives on a farm.
Near Swift Current, Saskatchewan where there is a lot of charm.
On it, one can find grasshoppers, ants and mice.
Sometimes species of caterpillars, bedbugs and lice.
But the insects don't do any real harm.
--
In Craik, Saskatchewan. Dan Fletcher, a local; businessman.
To Town Hall he ran,
With an inquiry
About his license expiry.
And was told: "Renew it quickly as you can."
--
In Carberry, Manitoba, Ted Swanson is a country land owner
Where the county clerk made a tax boner,
And apologised by saying, "Sir, here is your refund as a gift.
Which will give your concern a lift."
Land owner Ted was a loner.
--

The security man was calling.
"Although the wind is stalling,
Trees are uprooted and falling
Trucks a no longer hauling.
The scenery is appalling."
--
Abe, the, Selkirk, Manitoba hotel manager received a complaint from Mable occupying room # 42,
Furious, Mable said to the manager: "I have a complaint for you.
There are bed bugs in my room and I can't sleep so get me another room."
"O. K. the manager replied, "I'll get one soon.
For you, and your daughter too."
--
I'll bet you a wager.
That Mike who lives in Brandon, Manitoba won't marry her.
I suppose.
It's because of her titanic nose.
And only God can save her.
--

The Atlantic Ocean is gigantic.
The Pacific Ocean can be frantic.
Paris is great and so is New York.
Where one can enjoy a meal of either beef or pork.
This survey was conducted by statistician Orville Mantick.
--
In the Manitoba town of Portage La Prairie.
As soon as Harry Carrie
 Finished eating a blueberry. We got out of bed and there was fun galore.
While dancing on the new hardwood floor.
Every Saturday night in January.
--
Bobby, Bibby, peekaboo.
I wonder who made the poo?
Is it Joe, Moe?
Ho or Dar?
I want your name too.
--

Here are the latest **morning** news headlines. -
Palestinian Hamas is trying to eliminate the Jews.
Toronto Street People are short of shoes.
An EBOLA virus outbreak in Iberia.
1000 rebel terrorists killed in Syria
Because they had wrong views.
--
Here are the latest **noon** news headlines --
A Scandal the Tories Won't Shake.
President Obama says he had made a mistake.
Another Malaysian plane shot down in Ukraine.
A rebel revolution in Spain.
In Medicine Hat, a farmer finds a huge snake.
--
Here are the latest **evening** news headlines.--
A dispute continues between Israel and Hamas.
Russian Putin says, "I'm the boss.
 A flood in Croatia and earthquake in China.
A triple murder in Regina.
Lucky it wasn't one of us.
--

Here are the latest **Sports** headlines.--
Blue Jays lose to the Orioles again.
NHL hockey season soon to begin.
Edmonton Eskimos are in first place in the CFL.
Winnipeg Jets, NHL hockey coach mad as hell.
One wonders where the coach had been in.
--
Looking at the setting sun.
Can be lot of fun.
If your sun glasses fit you right.
You might.
Try to see the moon change places with the sun.
--
To tell you the truth.
What Brick Muth did in the Saskatchewan Town of Carrot River is uncouth.
When he had to go and pee.
 He unzipped his fly and did it by a tree.
So that everyone could see.
--

Weather forecasters below.
 Know:
That when the temperature reaches thirty below.
It probably will snow.
Much colder than a year ago.
--
In Ontario, the new taxes the government plans to amend.
Offends the taxpayers no end.
Because the province is in debt.
And residents haven't paid their property taxes yet.
And have their own bills to send.
--
The sky is blue.
So what is new?
Planet Earth will still exist.
Although with a mist.
If this statement isn't a lie, then it has to be true.
--

The winds had ceased.
And David Carlson from Manitoba's Stony Mountain Penitentiary has been released.
But David did not know.
Where to go.
Until, he met a parolee from the east.
--
In the Saskatchewan Town of Meadow Lake, Angie Moe was gutless.
Jenny Penny on the other hand was anemic and toothless.
Both for lack of money.
Were reluctant to go to the beach exposing stretch marks on their tummy.
Sometimes there is no justice and each agreed, Sometimes our lives are fruitless."
--
In the Manitoba town of Winkler, Wanda was strikingly youthful.
And beautiful.
To be truthful.
Her life wasn't fruitful,
As her behaviour was brutal.
--

In the Saskatchewan City of Moose Jaw, Jack Wynn had been in and out of love a 100 times in his life.
Attempting to find a loving and true wife.
First there was Mary, Canary.
Then Cherry and Carry.
Jack's life was a world of grief and strife.
--

In the Ontario city of Orillia, Ophelia was incredibly beautiful with blue eyes.
Privately she hoped that her ex dies.
Because he abused her day and night.
And always wanted to argue and fight.
The ex was also an expert at telling lies.
--

In a Cranbrook, B. C. Track and Field Meet, Rod was first and never wanted to be last.
He could jump high and run fast.
When the weather was hot.
When the weather was cold however, he could not.
Because after a cold blast, he was always harassed.
--

During the annual Niagara Falls Track and Field meet.
Athlete Rod looked into a mirror and saw his face that was sweet.
As he wanted to be the best.
 He ate several bananas and then had a rest.
After he had had washed his feet.
--
In Kitimat, B. C. during the Canada Winter Games there was Jim.
With a shark he decided to have a swim.
He patted its head.
After it was fed.
I wonder what happened to the shark and to Jim.
--
In the Saskatchewan town of Prince Albert, a car driver was nineteen.
One passenger was fifteen.
The other in between.
Although he was clean.
He was also mean.
--

In the British Columbia town of Dawson Creek.
Although meek.
At age twenty-three.
Jack climbed a Jack pine tree.
To see a robin that sang on the same tree every week.
--
Mark and Sweet.
After midnight went to a Stellerton, Nova Scotia street.
To have something to eat.
At a restaurant they ordered a cup of coffee and a sandwich made of meat.
Finished eating they sang a song, Eating Meat after Midnight is a Treat.
--
On the American television network NBC.
A Canadian political member from the NDP.
Discussed, climate change and oil pipe lines
The EBOLA outbreak, ISIS and African lions.
What their next topic will be, we will have to wait and see.
--

In the Saskatchewan town of North Battleford, to keep the rabbits at bay.
From eating a farmer's barn hay.
From the Hudson Bay is another way.
Is to place a mare that is colored bay.
Then the rabbits will be frightened and not want to stay.
--

In the Alberta community of Beaverdam,
Tessa Mam to Flo Lam. an email writes --
I don't give a damn. This isn't one of those guru work-at-home frights.
My dear, click here without fear for an unbelievable cash pay.
Grab it now if you want to make $2000 per day.
I'm not one that with a client shimmies and shakes, lies, argues and fights."
--

Abel and Grable dropped their eyes, and began to laugh.
One was a zoo monkey and the other a giraffe.
Both worked half on half.
With the zoo staff.
For their work schedule, they used a graph.
--

In the Saskatchewan town of Yorkton,
Evadne and Will.
Were celebrating their marriage on top of a hill.
They shared a bottle of wine,
Sent by a friend of mine.
The bride and groom were so excited that they couldn't keep still.
--
In British Columbia town of Creston, Harry Beston was strong and had a big fist.
With which he couldn't resist.
 Punching Arthur on head,
That bled.
Because Harry was suffering from liquor thirst.
--
In the California city of Santa Maria.
Tenor Rico Korea each Sunday morning use to sing Ave Maria.
Rico is thirty-three.
But looks like fifty-three.
And no longer sings because he gets frequent attacks of diarrhea.
--

Scantily.
Lives in Chile.
Who didn't understand anything,
Until she met Billy, who knew everything.
Although he too is young and silly.
--
As God is above.
We can freely talk about love.
And if you do not understand.
Give me your hand.
This will be done with the assistance of a dove.
--
I once loved Joe so much.
My heart would flutter with his touch.
Then he took my hand
And told me what he had planned,
And I said, "No Way because you are Dutch."
--
Harry McCook once had a cook.
Who took a soup recipe from a book.
But one day the soup turned out to be a gobblycook.
As he shook and shook.
As for the recipe he did not look.
--

For the 15 Plum Coulee, Manitoba working group.
Cook Jean with a swoop.
Made a vegetable soup.
When eaten most of the troop,
Had to go and poop.
--
"My grandpa Hank I never did see.
Before I was born, some say he had died while sailing on the sea.
Others say he was killed while riding a motorcycle that had crashed into an oak tree.
The information is old and new.
I don't know if either is true.
To find out I'll have to do more research from A to Z."
--
In the Saskatchewan village of Big River, I spent the day.
During the month of May.
Catching fish.
Enjoyed eating it from a dish.
However, I wish I could find enjoyment some other way.
 --

In the Alberta community of Paddle Prairie, lived Harry.
Who wanted to marry.
It was a lovely August evening.
The fresh air he was breathing.
Ideal for a canary.
--
In British Columbia town of Chilliwack, there is a lady by the name of Kay Ritter.
Who besides being a secretary is also a baby sitter.
Don proposed marriage.
And rented a 2 horse carriage.
A month later, Don was on a Caribbean cruise with her.
--
Coast to Coast AM is an overnight radio program hosted by George Noory.
After you listen to him you will not have to worry.
As topics include: UFOs, strange occurrences, colonizing Mars and life after death.
And other unexplained phenomena. Oh so much information of wealth.
If you are able, tune in, you will not be sorry.
--

The 1930s Great Depression was a severe worldwide economic depression.
That began in 1929 when the US economy first went into a recession.
The turning point and recovery came with the beginning of the Second World War.
When every major currency left the gold standard and United States entered the war and more:
The Depression and the recovery succession was a historic time for the world to freshen.
--
Adam Suntory is an Alberta Tory.
Who had a story.
About his girlfriend named Corrie,
Who said to Adam, "I'm sorry.
Instead of marrying you, I have married am Ontario Liberal, Laurie."
--
In Diefenbaker Lake, Saskatchewan, Carol Ritter is a pea picker.
That isn't a quitter.
When she picks peas.
She is a tease.
And hopes to become richer.
--

In Stellerton, Nova Scotia, Cushy Deane is an apple picker.
And picks apples that are only bigger.
She has a lovely figure.
And as a gold digger.
Is also a shipper and a sniffer.

--

Lack of sleep may lead to brain shrinkage.
And sleep is a linkage.
To stay in sync with nature.
Where reason is a stature.
Of the old vintage.

--

In the Alberta Aboriginal community of Fort Chipewyan, on a street corner,
Fred said to Ted.
"For our health reasons the Kearl Oil Sands project must not go ahead". Ted then said, "I agree the $12 billion project owners, Imperial Resources and Exxon Mobil must bend."
"Because it's a dread." Fred said.
Both shook hands and then fled.

--

"Get up! Get up!" shouted Hilda.
To Mathilda.
"Do not shout so loud," said Tilda.
Because you'll wake up Fidilda.
"Shut up all of you!" said Gilda.
--
A young Rapid City, Manitoba man while courting a girl.
 Met a squirrel whose name is Merle.
She is a pack rat.
Wearing a straw hat.
So the man gave her a swirl.
--
Anne in Alberta's town of Marwayne.
 First rode a plane.
Then a train.
Sunshine or rain.
Eventually she became insane.
--
"Is that you?"
Bawled Ivan Chochou.
"You are here too.
Feeling blue?
For coming. Thank you."
--

On TV.
The picture you see.
That is me.
On the sea.
With my daughter Lee.

--

I enjoy camping out.
Because I don't have to shout.
To my friends
Who understands
That I'm suffering with gout.

--

Ed had an influenza bug.
Bought himself a drug.
Put it into a mug.
Occupied by a frog.
Owned by my friend, Doug.

--

Early in the morning.
After he had been snoring.
Tenant Ed, to the landlord complained about a resident across the street.
Who had bare feet.
That the resident's cock wakes him up in the morning.

--

Tenant Jane says, "Mr. Landlord, would you do something about the man living on top of me every night.
I do not want to fight.
I don't think it's right.
But I might.
If it's alright?"

--

"Would you please have a look at my water?
It's causing havoc to me and my daughter.
Also I had the repairman down on the floor three times but he still didn't give me satisfaction.
He's a distraction.
As I'm getting hotter and hotter."

--

'Mr. Landlord, why are you claiming the cockroaches as my pets?
It's not a rule the Landlord Advisory Board sets.
Also, a stranger keeps knocking on my drawer at three in the morning.
My fright is sort of soaring,
And oh yes, how about the noise above, by the flying jets?"

--

In unit 3 their 18 -year old son Dick,
continually keeps banging his balls against the fence.
And per chance?
Can you repair my kitchen sink?
As my apartment is beginning to stink.
I leave you this note with no offence."

--

Disputes can arise between the landlord and the tenant.
Who at times has no parent.
A third party can hear both sides of the story.
In the end one or the other can say, "I'm sorry."
"Even if the tenant is a lieutenant."

--

If the Landlord/Tenant dispute is about accommodation, noise or pollution.
There is a solution.
The Private Residential Tenancies Board may help.
Without a yelp.
Or starting a tenant revolution.

--

In a Landlord/Tenant dispute if the parties concerned do not agree.
For free.
They have a 21 day cooling off period to either accept or reject a judicator's decision.
And in that time neither side can go fishing.
With you or me.
--

In New Brunswick there's a Landlord named Mann,
Who collects his monthly rent quickly as he can.
One month he began to snoop.
And after enjoying a bowl of soup.
Picked up the money and took a flight to Iran.
--

Apartment owner Dick Crosier.
On his 4 stories building had a foreclosure.
With composure.
He did not make a disclosure.
Dick received a notice with a foreclosure enclosure.
--

At Hanson Brothers, there are condo unit sales.
Built out of brick and steel nails.
You can buy one today.
And not pay until the end of May.
Phone for more details.

--

Brown and Sheet.
Have an apartment for rent that's a treat.
1200 square feet.
Tidy and neat.
Tenant pays his/her own heat.

--

Our condo is small.
But unlike Ford's recall.
One can't take it back.
When one finds a crack.
On the ceiling, floor or the wall.

--

A tenant in Edmonton.
Was having a lot of fun.
He caught a porcupine.
And let it hang on the landlord's clothes line.
This done, he played a game of badminton

-

Roberto Fernando.
Bought a condo.
It's airy and bright
With plenty sunlight.
On Spadina Street in Toronto.

--

Jack Turner bought a new house which was next to sky.
In the Rocky Mountains people wanted to know why?
One said, ``Maybe because it`s close to heaven."
Another, ``Maybe because it's near a 7-Eleven."
Everyone wondered: At 89 when Jack would die.

--

In the province of Quebec there's a landlord named Hamel.
Who wasn't doing that well.
He charged a high rent.
And when told, prospect Jim Bent,
Said, "Go to hell."

--

The Canadian economy has been tanked.
Deposits no longer are banked.
RBC, National, Scotia and Montreal.
And that/s not all.
There's also TD, CIBC and ATB that should be thanked.
--
"Canadian house prices are overvalued by 30 percent."
Warns Bank of Canada governor Polozo, during a Chamber of Commerce event.
There's a risk to the economy and a correction should occur.
That's for sure.
If not there will be discontent. Some will not be able to pay their rent and forced to live in a tent.
--
Amanda! Amanda!
There's no country like Canada!
During winter and summer.
Amanda can drive a Hummer
Or a 2-door convertible Plymouth Barracuda.
--

I have a question today.
Why should I pray?
Because I'm not gay.
No one did I betray.
And everything else is O. K.
--
It seems to happen all the time.
My 5-line limericks don't rhyme.
On Sunday the sun doesn't always shine.
Newscasts are headlined with all sorts of crime.
My name is Adam Bernstein.
--
In Saskatoon, Sam Ford.
Felt bored.
At the swimming pool he heard the lifeguard say. "Hey, you peed in the pool and can`t swim in it anymore!"
Ford says, "But others have peed in it before."
The response was, "True, but not from the diving board."
--

The other day Joe was diagnosed with cancer.
Smoking was the enhancer.
Sometimes 2 packages a day.
His health was fading away.
Cure – Chemotherapy was the answer.
--
It's fifteen past five.
I'm still alive.
Following a two-hour colonoscopy surgery.
And then taken to an adult nursery.
Where I have to learn how to overcome the pain and survive.
--
Following my surgery.
And having committed perjury.
Hating myself I leaned against a spruce tree.
And threw away my ring and my key.
On my 25th wedding anniversary.
--
In Edmonton, 40- year old Albert is a diabetic.
No longer photogenic.
To satisfy his sweet tooth.
Doctor Jonathan White told the truth:
"Stop eating food with high sugar levels or else you will not become athletic."
--

Canadian doctor Frederick Banting co-discovered insulin after he had become deeply interested in diabetes.
Also known as mellitus.
A group of diseases.
Which squeezes.
High blood sugar levels found in many of us.
--
Canadian doctor Frederick Banting received the Nobel Prize in Medicine in 1923.
And between you and me.
He also was an Arctic adventurer and a keen art painter of the sea.
His fame came when he co-discovered insulin at the University of Toronto,
And pronto,
Millions through the world because of insulin and Doctor B. are trying to be diabetes free.
--

Sugar you should not eat.
Even if you enjoy food that is sweet,
Sugar can cause kidney failure and contribute to hyper activity, anxiety and depression.
Also risk of a coronary disease and weekend defence against bacterial infection.
One should no cheat and eat sugar as it may cause diabetes so also be certain not to eat certain types of red meat.

--

What happens to your body when you stop eating sugar?
It's time to find a non-diabetic cooker.
It improves your health.
When you stop, it can increase your wealth.
You lose weight and can play a game of snooker.

--

Fit people are more fun.
In rain or sun,
Fit people are smart and snappy.
 Instead of being crappy and unhappy.
And instead of walking they can run.

--

At the Royal Alexandra Hospital in Edmonton it's almost midnight.
Where for an emergency consultation I'm introduced to Doctor Jonathan White.
And he greets me by saying, "How are you?"
I say, "Fine. Thank you."
Then he asks, "Joe, how do you feel?"
I say, "With my fingers but my health isn't ideal. Something isn't just right."

At the Royal Alexandra Hospital in Edmonton there's Doctor Johnathan White.
Who is my height and very bright.
Every time we meet, he asks, "How are you? How do you feel? Did you get over the recent flu?"
Dr. White takes good care of his patients, even if their pocket book is tight.
--
Then Doctor White says, 'Joe, here is a simple precaution for you.
To avoid the flu.
Vaccination and hand washing are the best defence against the sickness.
As it is in most in most illness.
If you have s cold, a chronic cough and sneeze. Stay home and nothing do."

Dr. White said: "Joe you have the flue.
You're breathing in glue.
Your fever is high.
So why don't you try.
A glass or 2 of your favorite brew?"

--

Dr. White said: "I hope you aren't serious.
And you, Joe, aren't delirious.
I hope you butt isn't in a sling.
And I wish you the best of everything.
And your health problem isn't mysterious."

--

Dr. White says. "Hey Joe, how is it going?'
And I say, "Well, the wind is still blowing.
And it's still snowing.
And the crows are crowing.
And wife Faye, is surgery undergoing."

--

I'm impressed with Doctor White.
A quick prescription he can write.
And meet me day or night.
Especially, when I have difficulty with a mosquito bite.
Dr. White is always upright.

--

I'm acknowledging a request –
Well, when Doctor White gives one a test.
He is much more to the point than the rest.
Especially, when it comes to a cardiac arrest.
Doctor White is the best.
--
Doctor White, please give me a pill.
That will give me a thrill.
After a sigh.
I can get high.
I'll wait untill the prescription you fill.
--
Dr. White said: "Joe. I know that you have had surgery in places not to mention.
And you have been gone for a long time with frustration.
You have been to see the clergy
Discussing your surgery which was an emergency
And needed your immediate attention.
--

Dr. White said: "Joe, I hope your infection isn't serious.
And you aren't delirious.
I trust your butt is no longer in a sling.
As I wish you the best of everything.
And your health problem isn't mysterious."
--
During Halloween a witch and a warlock had sex.
She went to see Doctor White for some checks
The doc said, "Oh dear.
Its herpes I fear!
And she has mixed up a hell of a hex."
--
Doctor White asked, "Joe, what do you do for a living?"
I hesitated and said, "I had a misgiving.
And now drive a bus shuttle."
The doc gave no rebuttal
So I felt the conversation I was winning.
--

Doctor White's scale tells no lies.
But for me 25 pounds I did rise.
The doc refused to believe.
And continued to deceive.
Until he noted my increase in size.

--

Doctor White.
Had me consolidate my sleep at night.
And made sure the bedbugs didn't bite.
Especially if it's still daylight.
And the said, "Joe, do what I say and you will be alright."

--

I went to see Doctor White without an appointment.
And I say. "Doc I must have sex. I need excitement."
The doc looks at me amazed and says, "Joe, having sex is only in your head."
No. Listen. If I don't have sex. I'll could find myself all day in bed."
So Doctor White says, "OK I'll try and save your life but you can have sex only with your wife, No excitement."

--

Surgeon Doctor White had an appointment with his operating nurse.
Along came Rita Wagner with a large purse.
They discussed Joe's colon cancer operation which is infected.
And his stomach should be dissected.
Needing a reverse operation, after undergoing chemo therapy, at age 83, Joe's health was getting worse.

--

"Doctor. Doctor!" Joe excitedly said, after falling on a ski hill.
"Look. I feel terribly ill."
In comes Doctor White and a nurse.
Measles." Says the doctor.
"Mumps." Says the nurse with the large purse.
For Joe a funeral hearse is waiting still.

--

To doctor White Joe said, "I found a bedbug in my bed.
Which has caused extreme pain to my head."
And the doc said:
"It's fortunate that you aren't dead,
Here's a prescription to fumigated your bed."

--

Who said that Joe is dead?
Maybe it's only in your head.
Maybe his sickness is your disease.
So put yourself at ease.
And go to bed.

--

You are 60, better prepare for your wake.
Too many candles to put on your birthday cake.
First it could be arthritis and glaucoma.
Then melanoma and carcinoma.
Next retirement and if lucky, enjoy a T-bone steak.

--

Thomas Dhal.
Strong and tall.
Had a fall.
After he had several drinks of alcohol,
And that's not all.

--

Slim Linn.
Is a friend of Doctor Jenifer Spratlin.
At AHS Edmonton department of oncology.
The doc utilizes the latest cancer scientology.
Once you are referred to her, you'll never have to make an apology to Linn.

--

Jenifer Spratlin is a MD.
A member of FRCPC.
If you have cancer that's the person you want to see.
No matter if you are a he or a she.
Take that advice from me.

--

Oncologist Dr. Spratlin is on my Heath Care Team.
Who is the prettiest MD I have ever seen.
In chemotherapy step three.
Between you and me.
Because of her, my hands always had to be washed with soap and remain clean.

--

Doctor Jenifer Spratlin graduated as a MD (University of Alberta) in 2001.
Since then has been on the run.
At the Edmonton Cross Foundation since June 2012 as an oconologist
On a cancer research project.
Since then in cancer research, Jenifer has hit a home run.

--

Alex Koloda.
While going through cancer chemotherapy was prescribed the drug Xeloda.
The side effects are: vomiting, sores in the mouth and throat and Nausea.
Also: fatigue, immobility, depression and diarrhea.
Cancer is on the increase throughout Alberta.
--
A medical professional who practices oconology is an oconologist.
A professional who treats mental disorders is a psychiatrist.
One who doesn't believe in God is an atheist.
One who travels a lot is a tourist.
People who have no money are called, the poorest.
--
When my cancer chemotherapy was done.
Oconologist Jenifer Spratlin said: "Joe, a difficult time you have overcome.
And won!
Now you can go home to Faye, your loved one.
Relax in the sun, have fun, or go for a run."
--

Asthma symptoms are a reversible air flow.
Affecting any Joe.
Who is wheezing, has chest tightness,
coughing and short of breath.
And if not diagnosed in time may cause death.
That is happened to Lady Macbeth.
--
Asthma is on its strongest rise.
No matter if one has brown or blue eyes.
Dumb or wise.
It's no surprise.
Asthma affected millionaire Benjamin Wise.
--
Policeman. Policeman. Do your duty.
To help Barbara, a cutie.
Post man. Postman. You too do your duty,
By delivering my letter to Barbara, my beauty.
Both of you must imply your sense of duty,
--

In Toronto the CN Tower is 2660 feet tall.
And that's not all.
It's the tallest free-structure in the Western Hemisphere.
To reach the top some experience anxiety and fear.
Other interesting structures in Toronto are the Skydome and Eaton's Shopping Mall.
--
Three. Six. Nine the Canada goose drank wine.
A monkey chewed a banana on the street car line.
A lion chocked.
A penguin croaked.
Then all went to heaven in a row boat made out of binder twine.
--
Mable. Please set the table.
Just as fast as you are able.
And after you dine.
And enjoy a glass of wine
 You and Miss Grable hurry to the horse racing stable.
--

When I have money.
I enjoy a sardine sandwich with honey.
I have done this all my life.
Without the use of a knife.
To you this may sound funny.
--
I know Ted who is double- jointed
I give him a kiss but he's disappointed.
He has Pinocchio's nose
And Beaver-like toes.
To see Ted one needs an appointment.
--
I know a lady.
That always says, "Maybe."
She is a single Miss,
That loves to kiss.
Watch out! She's also a bit shady.
--
I went downtown.
To see Miss Brown.
She gave me a nickel.
To buy a dill pickle.
As soon as I laid my suitcase down.
--

For my copier I bought a cartridge of ink
Soon it began to stink.
Not that it wasn't clean.
But a customer near me.
Was vomiting into a sink.
--
Turn to the East. Turn to the West.
And choose the one you like the best.
The lady in blue and the other in red.
One with a necklace around her neck The other with blonde hair on her head.
The reply was: "Neither. I like a woman with a big chest."
--
In Liberia, 20 - year old Eric.
Is caught in the EDOLA an authentic epidemic.
A virus disease that already has claimed more than 5000 West African lives.
It strikes all sorts of people: children husbands, mothers and wives.
Like the 1918/1919 Spanish flu, because of EBOLA there's a world panic.
--

Happiness is that of a blissful state of mind.
The product of love the first time.
Recognize when you have it.
With both hands grab it.
Or else you'll be left behind.
--
Joe from Kokomo.
Head to toe.
Was always fashion dressed when playing the piccolo.
Near the belly button below.
A sign reads: Joe's Fashion and Piccolo show.
--
Poh and Vho have fast food restaurants in Cologne.
And Sierra Leone.
Both restaurants are well known.
However, at both, it's best not to dine alone.
For fear you will be hit by a stone.
--
Often I get asked on the phone:
Dad, the car broke down, how do I get home?
Can I order an iPad in more than one tone?
Why your credit card signature isn't shown?
Which waitress do you prefer – Sharon or Joan?
--

On the phone the most common questions I get asked are:
How are you?
And Are you a Jew?
Do you always say thank you?
What's new?
Is your favorite color blue?
--

Some people like the idea of mixing and matching.
Example – mixed marriage, a couple is sampling.
Baseball player - catching and pitching.
Concert audience - clapping and booing.
City Hall – between staffing and taxing.
--

Please. Help me to write a limerick!
What other words are there that rhyme with Limerick.
Besides: Critic, Cynic, Gimmick.
Lyric, Rhetoric
Dominic.
And Pinprick?
--

In the British Columbia town of Castlegar,
"Why are you so far unhappy?" asks Jim.
Liza says, "To see you and not the right to call him".
Liza was a fool to think.
That him was a dink.
A week later however, she was hugging and kissing him.
--
In the Newfoundland-Labrador town of Gander pretty Jane Keller from home ran away.
She refused to stay.
And next day to her father she texted a note.
And wrote:
"Dad, don't be afraid because I'll be home right away."
--
In the Alberta community of Fairview.
An old man that I knew.
Bought himself an antique car.
Then he went into a bar, to smoke a cigar.
When he returned the vehicle was missing and all he could do is say, "Dearest car, au revoir from my view."
--

Author Diller
Wrote a thriller
About a killer
Who was a miller
And also a whisky distiller
--
Mark Stone is a book critic.
But some say he is a cynic.
He gives a book review.
That is published and new.
His review is accepted only by few.
--
In the Alberta First Nations community of Fort McKay (pronounced mik-eye), a resident by the name of Cy.
Wanted to try.
To teach a young Canada goose.
That was on the loose.
How to fly so that it wouldn't constantly cry.
--

Some of the benefits working for a government are:
One doesn't have to always have their own car.
Vacation time one month and Retirement pension is great. One doesn't have to lose weight.
Or have to be honest or straight.
Working for the government the benefits are the best by far.
--
City Hall complaints:-
Taxes are too high.
Too much pollution in the sky.
Photo radar is a grab-cash.
Many drunken drivers crash,
News fed to the media sometimes is a lie.
--
Other City Hall Complaints:
Barking dogs.
Noisy frogs.
Poor sewers and sidewalks.
A Mayor that too much talks.
Councillors who believe they are saints.

What can I say?
Well, today is Tuesday.
The second of May.
And I'm not gay.
For that I say, Hooray!"

--

What else can I say?
Well, my wife's first name is Kay.
We mostly shop at the Bay.
Live in a chalet.
Where we live and play.

--

Is there anything else you want to say?
Yes. I have a substantial pay.
I enjoy eating at a buffet.
My wife, Kay, has passed away.
Otherwise everything else is O. K.

--

I know little about the animal Armadillo.
The same with the dish, Picadillo.
An Armadillo loves to sleep by a willow.
A Picadillo (in the Philippines giniling) is at times is difficult to swallow.
In both instances earthlings say, "Oh, Oh. Where is this city called Iloilo?"

--

Why should we be alarmed?
Because of pollution Planet Earth is no longer charmed.
In the Middle East, Christians are harmed.
In many countries good soil is no longer farmed.
And terrorist countries haven't been disarmed.
--
Yesterday I received an email.
It was from Arthur Dale.
Who had served time in jail.
For harming a Humpback whale.
Breaking laws that prevail.
--
Our son Dick.
Because of his physique.
Isn't a geek or a pipsqueak.
Every afternoon he has a leek.
And can speak English, French and Greek.
--
In the Yukon town of Watson Lake, Bob is a store clerk.
One day he came late to work.
Looking like a slob.
And lost his job.
Because he was a jerk.
--

Wikipedia.
A free internet encyclopedia.
For information.
From each nation.
What a wonderful social media.
--
Most people are polite.
When they write.
At any site.
Even where mosquitoes bite.
It's all right.
--
When at the University of Alberta, Dale.
His Doctorate Degree he did fail.
He hightailed to pick up his co-vivant Abigail.
And then, rushed to pick up his mail.
To see if his passport had arrived so they could travel to Bloomingdale.
--
In the British Columbia town of Hope.
There was an Outer Space creature that had a rope.
He had a horrible face.
And always wanted to race.
Every time that he washed himself with water and soap.
--

In the vibrant Manitoba town of Flin Flon,
lived Gus.
Who while riding to Winnipeg on a
Greyhound bus.
Didn't have a penny.
Until he met a passenger named Jenny.
They sat next to each other and promised not
to cuss.

--

Farmer's Weather Forecast--   (1)
Red sky in the morning.
Farmer takes warning.
Red sky at night.
A farmer's delight.
Grain prices to be broadcast.

--

Hens scratching dirt.   (2)
With rain farmer will flirt.
Summer fog.
Will scorch farmer's hog.
Find water to squirt.

--

When there is dew on the grass.   (3)
Rain will never come to pass.
A strong north wind says storm at night.
A strong west wind farmer will be alright.
No need to scratch someone's ass.

A drop in the barometer pressure.　(4)
Farmer gets a headache which isn't a pleasure.
Circle around the sun.
Cold weather will come.
Farmer will not treasure.
--
Bright full moon.　(5)
Favourable weather soon.
Seagulls flying in a flock.
Bad weather for the stock
If so, no time to croon.
--
Farmer hears thunder.
He begins to wonder.(6)
If hail will follow.
To disrupt his summer fallow.
Or was it a blunder?
--
A storm will soon pass. (7)
Alas.
Weather 20 below.
It probably it will soon snow.
Farmer needs money to buy gas.
--

When the rooster crows (8)
It's a sign market money flows.
When the crow arrives.
Time to start honey beehives.
That's the way farming goes.

--

The city of Toronto you are in trouble.
After viewing the city landscape on Google Earth and telescope Hubble.
There is something wrong with your soil.
Which makes me boil.
Because Hog Town may soon become a puddle.

--

The clown.
Jimmy Browne
Came to town,
To take part in a Camrose hoedown.
Where he was warned not to screw around.

--

A Dauphin, Manitoba, golfer named Anna Monroe.
Wanted to make more dough.
So she was going to turn pro.
To change her flow and go.
However, she suddenly changed her mind and married a wealthy Winnipeg beau.

Pretty Florence who is wise,
Has eyes unique in color and size.
When she opens them wide.
People turn aside.
Startled with surprise.
--
There was an American tourist.
Who was a purist.
He craved for a Canadian beer.
So it was brought to him by one of Santa's a reindeer.
When done, he drove to Radium Hot Springs with a balloonist.
--
Fernandez came from Peru.
Who I knew.
When he arrived in Canada he didn't know what to do.
Accidently he got into a fight with a bear.
Fernandez lost his hair.
Since he was nearly baldheaded he smiled and said, "Whoo! Whoo!"
--

A concert conductor in Rio.
Fell in love with Cleo.
As he was taking down her panties.
She said: "No or else I'll tell my aunties.
And live with them in Sacramento."
--
When Canada's Mr. Koon.
Visited Rangoon.
At noon.
There was a typhoon.
Which the Natives shun.
--
The Africa link.
Is on the brink.
Of falling apart.
With little heart.
For those in the pink.
--
When in Africa I visited Zambia.
Liberia, Ghana and Somalia.
In the 4 countries the economy is bursting.
Football games are rusting.
What else can I tell ya?
--

When I was courting Anesthesia.
We visited Philippines, Thailand and Malaysia.
That is warm and friendly. A melting pot of all religions and races.
Towering skyscrapers look down at many places.
To love Malaysia, one should visit all of Asia.
--
In Ottawa parliament was discussing turmoil throughout the world.
While Canadian curlers including Edmonton's Kevin Martin, and those throughout the world, curled.
Russia's Putin at the world hurled.
The UN tried to have his actions unfurled.
As the entire world swirled.
--
There was an athlete from Crete.
Who was attending an Okanagan Track and Field Meet.
Since he arrived in Canada he had plenty to eat.
But competitors began to cheat.
He did well despite the extreme Okanagan heat.
--

There was a man from Portugal who in
Toronto had a bakery.
Another operated a Spadina Street steakery.
Both agreed to climb up a tall oak tree.

To see if they could see the sea.
Both fell down. One became an amputee and
the other harmed his knee.

--

Heinz Stout.
Is a Kraut.
In and Out.
He has to pout.
About his sauerkraut.

--

Confucius disciple Bu Shang helped to write
the classic book **I Ching**.
To many people happiness he did bring.
That was thousands years ago.
When the world economy was slow.
And reading a book didn't mean a thing.

--

In China the book **I Ching** remains a widely used divination text today.
No one can take China's history away.
The book has influenced countless philosophers and even business people's.
Including Western thinkers and artists like the Beatles.
The book is on and Amazon website but if you want to read it you have to pay.
--
In China there`s a man named Kou.
Who I knew.
And he introduced me to Avatar Pi
And then to Lin Kuei.
And his brother Lou.
--
Young Jen Yu.
First was in love with Ming Sui
And then Hen Kai
And still later My Pie
And ended marrying Chin Kou.
--
Tin Koo.
Was in love with Sun Wu.
And was doing well with enthusiasm.
Until he had an orgasm.

And their friendship was through.In Selkirk, Manitoba lived a Finn.
Who had a long chin.
He made it look sharp.
While he played the harp.
Sometimes he couldn't remember when to begin.
--
Bill, worked at a sawmill.
Situated near a Sicamous, B. C. steep hill.
Seldom, if ever, did he standstill.
Sometime he would run up and down with brother Will.
Until one night he had a spill and then felt ill.
--
In Melfort, Saskatchewan, Rex had most unusual behavior.
In many ways he was a failure.
When able.
He would sleep on a table.
And then pray to Our Savior.
--
Kenny.
Never had a penny.
He spent all his money.
It may sound funny.
But he spent it on his honey bunny, Jennie.

Near the city of Vancouver.
Hank rushed through a field of clover.
But large bees.
Stung his knees.
And his adventure was over.
--

In the Vancouver Chinese community of Chunking.
There was a man who was amazing.
He had a rickshaw.
For his pa and ma.
Who while driven, felt like a queen and king.
--

A young soldier returned home Afghanistan.
And in Richmond B. C, met pretty Sally Anne.
Who thought the soldier was a charmer without armour.
And wouldn't harm her.
She wanted to marry him as quickly as she can.
--

A curvaceous model in Vancouver.
During a fashion show did cover.
Her boobs with books.
So when the audience looks.
No one would recognize her

In British Columbia there was a young man in in the town Terrace.
Whose name was Hugh Harris.
He could dance the polkas and the jigs.
After eating hundreds of figs.
And no one did he embarrass.
--
In the British Columbia city of Vernon.
There was a lad whose name was Jimmy McKiernan.
After eating sauerkraut for an hour.
That was sour.
He decided to learn how to speak German.
--
One day me and my friend Rupert.
Went deep-sea fishing in British Columbia's Prince Rupert.
We caught several salmon, a halibut and other fish.
Which we then put into our boat dish.
But the fish escaped while we were listening to music composed by Franz Schubert.
--

While in southern Spain I stopped in the city of Cadiz.
Where most travellers know where it is.
While talking with a merchant's daughter.
I fell into puddle of water.
Wondering what a strange situation this is?
--
Once there was a boy named Dan McCann.
Video games his mother did ban.
She made him boiling mad.
Never worse day he had.
So he picked up his jacket and away from home he ran.
--
In Humboldt, Saskatchewan there was a guy named Stan Mann.
Who had trouble being a man.
He wore a dress and high heels.
Drove a Ford with pink wheels.
And soon Stan became a Tran.
--

In the Saskatchewan community of Indian Head.
There was a newspaper item that read:
"Resident discovered a human head in a box.
It definitely did not belong to a fox.
No one knows whose it is, but before being put into a box it bled."
--
An elderly self-centered Flin Flon man named Keith.
Sat down on his false teeth.
Said he for a start:
"Oh Lord bless my heart!
As I have bitten myself underneath.``
--
George Halbour.
Is my neighbour.
Who one day asked me for a favour.
And says, "My wife is in labour.
Can your wife please come and help her?"
--
My neighbour Alex Cooper.
Is a snooper.
He snoops to see if I ever lived in Texas.
And if I had paid my taxes.
In the neighbourhood he is also known as a nosey pooper

From Edmonton to the oil sands near Fort McMurray there's Highway 63.
Which is dangerous and tragic as can be.
Between you and me, let's agree.
The highway is more dangerous than sailing on a rough sea.
For either a he or a she.
--

YOUR HOROSCOPE REPORT

January

Coldest moth of the year-- Watch your ears don't get frozen. – You may have disastrous results.

February

Shortest month of the year – A ground hog to appear – You are especially friendly.

March

There won't be anything spectacular in your life – If single good time to find a wife.

April

There will be lots of ups and downs -- Easter is here -- Lots of rain. – Listen for strange sounds.

May

Your life will be more passionate, -- Easy to get depressed. -- Don't hesitate.

June
Good time to watch the moon – Marriage proposal soon – Be careful who you swoon.
July
You are pushing your creativity – Enjoy your vacation. --You'll experience sensitivity.
August
No official holiday –Time for reflection. -- Watch for specials at the Bay. During an election
September
You are understanding – Need money for education. – Time to do some remembering.

.   October
Your relationship will be sensitive – Think positive – Be creative and kind to a Native.

November
Your energy flows. -- Be prepared for a snow storm. -- Watch election results and if to a casino your husband goes.
December
Because of world turmoil Santa may not come this Christmas. -- Watch your credit card – Your life goes into overdrive. While you drive through an isthmus.

During the month of **January.**
Tom and Cherry.
Did marry.
For their honeymoon the traveled to Sudbury.
Where at a commissary, they enjoyed a dish of huckleberry.

--

During the month of **February.**
Jack was in the military.
Wife, Patricia, was a missionary.
Both often used a dictionary.
In some instances their views were contrary.

--

My friend John March.
During the month of **March.**
Thought he was a scholar.
In search of the value of a Canadian dollar.
He stopped searching as soon as he found a package of corn starch.

--

Arnold Staple.
During the month of **April.**
Had a television set but no cable.
Since he was unable.
He sat at a table and enjoyed a cup of tea with Miss Grable.

--

During the month of **May.**
For farmer Jay, it was time to cut his hay.
While cutting the mower broke down.
To have it repaired, he took it to town.
Where he said, "This seems to happen each May.``

--

During the month of **June.**
In the forenoon.
Mr. Gloom decided to take a trip to Rangoon.
But then decided it was too soon.
So he enjoyed himself at a saloon.

--

During the month of **July.**
I asked myself, "Why is it that I cry?
Is it because I drink and get high?
My, My, My!
Dear Lord, please tell me why?"

--

During the month of **August.**
Nap was a chemist – Pap a druggist.
Nap sexiest – Pap funniest.
Nap an egoist – Pap a nudist.
To this day it hasn't been determined who is the craziest.

--

Last year during the month of **September.**
Buddy was a member of the Community Centre.
Friend Cody was in the town of Grand Centr
Buddy was a casino spender.
Cody was an aldermanic contender.
Later, both had dementia and couldn't remember.
--
During the month of **October.**
Will Roper.
While sober.
Drove his Rover.
Went to a casino and stayed drunk until the poker game was over.
--
Early in **November.**
Ben became a member.
Of the German Shepard Dog Club.
During a heavy fog.
Taking care of the dog he did not surrender.
--
And now it's the month of **December.**
Forever I must remember.
Christmas day is coming.
Cash registers are humming
Even during stormy weather.

At the British Columbia Kootenay Lake, lived a boater named Sam.
Who when he was stuck in a jam.
Jumped from his boat.
And stayed afloat.
Until he went over the WK dam.
--
There was a traveler who stopped in Quebec.
And spoke only in Czech.
He could not speak French.
Overcoming a stench he sat down on a bench,
Where he strained his neck, His visit became a wreck.
--
A young couple set out on a trek.
Through the Laurentian Mountains of Quebec.
All went well.
 Until the found a hotel.
And then all they wanted to do is neck.
--
In the Quebec Laurentian Mountains lived a squirrel named Steven.
Whose teeth were sparkling and even.
But then the squirrel had rabies.
And got rid of her babies.
That's when I said, "I'm leaving."

When I attended a pilgrimage in the Quebec town of Sainte Ann-de-Beaupre.
I met an invalid by the name of Jean Beauvais.
At the Basilica I showed him a copy of Michelangelo's Pieta.
For which he said, "Ta-Ta."
The Basilica is also a place of miracles where people on crutches come and pray.

--

In the Quebec University of Laval.
Was a student by the name pf Rene LaSalle.
Who wanted a clear vision of the future.
He didn't want to be a butcher.
So for additional information he attended a medicine ball.

--

In the Quebec town of Sherbrooke during nights and days.
The card game, cribbage, Yvonne plays.
With companions 2 and 4.
And sometimes even more.
In each game, Yvonne always the competition slays.

--

In the Quebec town of Gatineau, Lucien Perrault, in stature was minute.
But he could shoot.
And play the flute.
The truth:
He could do both the best when he wore his Sunday suit.

--

In the Quebec community of Deux Montagnes, lives vegetarian Monsieur Rex.
A beef meal he rejects.
He enjoys his vegetables and herbs.
His appetite he curbs.
Slimmer and slimmer he gets.

--

In Quebec, everyone except moi.
Speaks French that they call Quebecois.
I just sat there with a grin.
 While eating my poutine.
'Cause Francais je ne parle pas.

--

In Gatineau, Quebec, Student Jean Luc
His head was always in a book.
It wasn't about former premier Pauline Marois.
Or former Canadien goalie Patrick Roy.
He was trying to learn how to be a cook.

Tammy Hall.
Lives in Montreal
Owns a stuffed doll
She had purchased at a shopping mall.
The doll fell of a wall and now cannot crawl
--
2014 was the year Quebec experience a construction corruption.
In Alberta there was a year of an oil boom destruction.
Guns kill more people than cars in Canada
Canada's senate loses its stamina
Because of its scandal disruption.
--
On January 11, 2015 people in Canada commemorated Canada's first Prime Minister Sir John a Macdonald's 200th birthday.
There were parties from BC to PEI and far away.
Sir John was the only Canadian Prime Minister to resign over a scandal.
But as a crafty politician he knew how to handle.
Negotiations for Confederation which exists to this day.
--

In the Alberta town of Taber, Garry likes to eat corn and to bet.
He even did it on the net.
Then one day.
The money went away.
And now Garry is drowning in debt.
--
There is a woman in the Alberta town of Clyde.
Who fell in the outhouse and died.
Next day her brother.
Fell in the other.
And now they are in turd side by side.
--
In the B. C. city of Nanaimo, Louis Mayo purchased vegetable seeds.
For all his garden needs.
However, eventually it came to pass.
There were no vegetables, only grass.
And a whole bunch of weeds.
--
The publishing of a book.
By author C, C, Cook.
One year it took.
Because the publisher was a crook.
And Cook first forgot to a publisher look.
--

In the Manitoba town of Mendoza.
Rosa Petrosa at one time lived in Minnesota.
She first hooked up with Kevin Barboza.
Then Domenico Somoza.
But ended marrying Carozza Zargoza-Spinoza.
--

In the Manitoba town of Morden, there lived a wild deer named Buck.
To a garden each night he snuck.
And waited all night.
Until the time was right.
He then jumped over a fence and was hit by a drunk-driven truck.
--

In Winnipeg there was a man with devices.
His ears were different sizes.
One ear was small.
The other he did not use at all.
But it won him several prizes.
--

In Winnipeg there's a lady who came from Ukraine.
Every day it gets cold she feels an arthritic pain.
She goes to a drug store.
And to a clerk says, "My knees are sore.
On my health chart, arthritis is quite a strain."
--
A young lady who immigrated to Winnipeg from Wales.
Says, "A strange odor in our house prevails.
During the night.
She searched the house with a flashlight.
And found empty stinky, garbage pails.
--
In Winnipeg.
Our neighbor Meg
In a nearby brook
Caught 2 fish on the same hook.
As she stood on one leg.
--

A lady who immigrated to Manitoba from Zambesi.
One day said, "Attracting Canadian men is easy.
I meet them in Winnipeg when it's breezy.
But not if the men are sneezy.
Otherwise I meet them even if the weather is freezy."

--

There was an elderly man in Manitoba's Lake Lynn.
Who married two widows who had been.
Asked why not a third:
The reply was: "How absurd?
Didn't you know that bigamy is a sin?"

--

In the Alberta town of Oyen, there was a man named Y. N. Shaw.
Who always wore a mackinaw and envied his maw and paw.
To share their life.
He found himself a wife.
And became his own father-in-law.

--

There was a young lady in the B. C. town of Oliver.
Where a whole bunch of young men used to follow her.
Until a man named Guy came along.
And sang her a favorite love song.
Since then the other men stopped following her
--
In the Newfoundland-Labrador town of Bonavista, there was a little creature.
Who had an unusual feature.
He had flown in from Mars.
To raid all the Bonavista bars.
This done he was congratulated by a preacher.
--
In Labrador City and nearby Wabush there is sadness.
And even madness.
Because iron ore mining has come almost to an end.
And many a friend.
Near the Quebec border is experiencing an economic crash and unhappiness.
--

Skip to my Lou.
And then to my sister Sue.
If you want to find what is new.
In finding a brew.
That is enjoyable by me and you.
--
Oh dear, what can the matter be?
Since we went for that drink of tea.
And on the way back got stung by a bee.
And for me,
It's now difficult to see.
--
Things are going great.
When I wasn't still awake.
And thought I was enjoying a juicy steak.
But I made a mistake.
What I was really enjoying was a piece of chocolate cake.
--
This is an exciting day in Milwaukee.
For Bob, the local disc jockey.
That is stocky.
To see the game of hockey.
Featuring Sydney Crosby.
--

Clarence McCain.
Has a problem with his brain.
He can't go to Spain.
Again.
Because this time he has a pulmonary vein.
--
Mitch.
Says, "Which.
One makes the right pitch.
Can become rich.
Without consulting a witch."
--
Hoydee.
Toydee.
Today is Sunday.
Tomorrow is Monday.
Both work days for me.
--
After a tete- a-tete
In our state.
In our office not to hate
Anyone that comes late.
Searching for a mate.
--

Tom didn't know what to do.
So he purchased a Skidoo.
And after a review
He purchased two.
Both are brand new.
--
Don is accused.
And not amused.
For a charge of sexual abuse.
Using a noose.
And that the complainant was bruised.
--
What's on in Edmonton.
That is for fun?
Upcoming is the 3 mile run.
And when this done.
One can interview Theresa who is famous nun.
--
In Illinois.
Andre Roy.
Is Mama's baby boy.
Fun to watch and enjoy.
Although he is a bit coy.
--

There's an eagle near the sky.
That dropped a poop into my eye.
I wondered why,
And did not cry.
Just glad that cows cannot fly.
--
Anna's college math lessons were split.
She did well in arithmetic.
Which was free
But she failed in geometry.
Which cost her a bit.
--
When Ed was younger he owned an MGA sports car.
That took him far.
One day he accidently hit jaywalker Rusty Mihar.
A musical star.
Well known for playing the guitar.
--
When Jim lived in B. C.s town of Hope
He bought himself a skipping rope.
Had a ginger ale.
And was put into jail.
For believing he was the Pope.
--

My name is Alice.
And I live in a palace,
My husband's name is Arthur.
And he thinks he's General MacArthur.
With a large phallus.
--

A Kentucky chicken jumped inside a tire.
That caught on fire.
It was too hot.
So she jumped into a large pot.
Which was her initial desire.
--

When your birthday comes.
I'll order a basket of plums
When your anniversary comes, I'll order peaches
When eaten it will make us.
Not to become bums.
--

On my grandfather's farm.
Usually there is no harm.
In the barn.
But darn.
Why this morning there was an alarm?
--

When Rene was in France.
To teach ladies how to do the modern dance.
First the heel and hen the toe.
Spin around and out you go.
And then, one may want to begin a romance,

--

I like coffee. Sarah likes tea.
The boys like me
And the girls like he.
And maybe
For once we'll agree.

--

I buy bubble gum, loony a packet.
The carton. I crack it.
When I blow, I don't make a racket.
As I'm a student in the upper bracket.
When I'm finished blowing bubbles,. The
packet I but put into my jacket.

--

Christopher Columbus sailed the ocean blue.
Discovering North America in 1492.
I don't know if that is true.
Between me and you.
Some say the Vikings were in Canada before 1492.

--

Janet was dressed in yellow.
When she was enjoying Jell-O.
That was mellow.
As she was playing her cello.
And then kissing her fellow.
--
I made a mistake.
When I was enjoying a sponge cake.
And began to shake
When approached by a snake.
And said: "What is tis for goodness sake?"
--
In our flower garden grows.
A pretty red rose.
That is sweet
Prettiest on the street
If not attacked by the hungry crows.
--
In the Alberta town of Viking there was Kyle.
Who lived like a king and loved to smile.
One day he went to the fair.
 Where he got bitten by a bear.
Now there is a lawsuit file.
--

In the B. C. town of Abbottsford, near a fjord,
there was a cute little bunny.
Who the proprietor thought was funny.
After Bunny had eaten several carrots.
He began talking to the parrots.
On days that became sunny.
--
In the Alberta town of Nanton,
There was a boy named Anton.
That became blue.
After he sniffed glue.
Like he use to do when he lived in Scranton.
--
In the Alberta farming community of Bellis I met a pretty lady from Dallas.
Who seemed to be very poor and her name was Alice.
A week later she went to a casino and won a great sum.
But accidently fell on her bum.
Thus not having her wish to be glamorous.
--

In the Alberta resort town of Lake Louise, there was a tourist named Bill.
Who had a fancy for receptionist named Jill.
But she liked him not.
For he was a sneezer and full of snot.
So tourist Bill got nil and eventually connected with Sil.
--
In the Alberta community at Bear Trap Lake, there was a frog named Cog.
Who liked to sit on a lily pad and then on a log.
One day because of a cough.
It slipped off.
And now its in the bog with a hog.
--
In the Alberta town of Taber, Don has a fear.
Because he tried growing corn in his ear.
When the temperature rose.
He would blow his nose.
Now popping is all he can hear.
--

There was a man living in the Saskatchewan town of Hudson Bay.
Who was bald and wore a toupee.
Although it was dumb.
He stuck out his thumb.
And the wind blew the toupee away.
--
There was an insurgent in Afghanistan.
Who was scheming to carry out a plan.
But he got shot.
On the spot.
As the UN wanted to stop the war as quickly as it can.
--
In the Alberta town of Marwayne, this may sound insane, but there is a deep moat.
Live a chicken, a duck and a goat.
When they wanted to go out.
They would wonder about.
Until they find a boat.
--
In the Alberta hamlet of Entwistle.
Derrek had a whistle
As a professional
He went to a confessional.
Penance was too diet, not to riot and remain sensational.

In the Alberta town of Hinton.
Lived pretty Shelly Minton.
Who each time she ate a zucchini.
She wore a colorful bikini.
It made her friends terribly mad and her mother sad until she had a martini and married
Albert Brinton.
--

In British Colombia's city of Prince George, near a gorge, lives a construction framer.
By the name of Chris Kramer.
Who is divorcing his wife of 2 years.
Because of continuous fears.
That she is a no-brainer.
--

Paulo Fernandez lives in Cuba.
And oh, how he can play the tuba.
Even as he suffers from tuberculosis.
And thrombosis.
Paulo is also skilful in diving using a scuba.
--

Cheng Wong.
Lives in Hong Kong.
In a tour package of three days and two nights.
By an ocean liner or airline flights.
One can also watch Cheng, an expert, in playing ping-pong.

--

I wish I was still single.
Then my pockets would jingle.
No more caring for a wife.
 Which has been a struggle all my life.
And then I'd have the freedom to go and mingle.

--

Don`t let life let you down.
So get up and leave town.
It won`t be hard.
 To keep you on guard.
As you can turn your life around.

--

Joy McCoy
And her friend Roy.
Their visit we enjoy.
When they bring a toy.
For Ben. our baby boy.

--

The graceful whooping crane is North America's largest bird.
It's an endangered species that is observed.
There are about 600 remaining throughout the world while the Canadian Wood Buffalo and U. S/Arkansas flock remains at about 278.
There could be more provided they mate and aren't harmed by a buffalo herd.

--

The other day I was bird watching and spotted a snowy owl.
I was so excited I let out a howl.
Snow owls live most of the time near the Arctic.
When I saw one in my yard I was enthusiastic.
The owl stayed for an hour and flew away without me committing a fowl.

--

Butterfly. Oh, Butterfly.
You have almost become extinct and that has made me cry.
Your brightly colored wings are missed.
And I cannot resist.
To ask, your absence, if it's not because of pesticides, than please tell me the reason why.

--

Donald is a hippie.
From Mississippi.
Who is kind of lippy.
And creepy.
And everyone says he is also a bit shitty.

--

Sam Plotnikoff's Barbershop in the B. C. town of Grand Forks opens at 9 o'clock.
At which time he takes stock.
And kills a fly that is on the wall.
Minutes later, customers' come. Some are short and some are tall.
And the Barbershop suddenly becomes a gossip centre similar to the Russian Community Hall that closes at 11 o'clock.

--

Leaving Montreal on the VIA Rail Canadian train sat a pretty lady, intoxicated.
As the train moved towards Toronto she became saturated.
Later agitated.
And then constipated.
Thus at noon, her time for dinning, she abdicated.

--

In Glasgow, Nova Scotia there was a truck driver name Laurie.
Who forever kept saying, I'm sorry.``
While driving a gravel truck.
One day he ran out of luck.
And ended upside down in a quarry.
--
Across Canada there's a drugstore chain called Rexall.
Where without a prescription one can purchase Tylenol.
Aside filling prescriptions, the chain also markets beauty products, baby diapers.
Elastic support, eye drops, itching powder and face wipers.
The swift service Rexall provides, one loves best of all.
--
Each day that pretty Anne.
Sat on the bathroom can.
She put on the fan.
Then on the internet began searching for a mate man.
Once she finds one, she has a tan.
--

In order to become Independent.
Kay appears resplendent.
She had a beautiful face.
But her demeanour was a disgrace.
She never could become a superintendent.

--

A young schizophrenic named Struther.
Was told of the death of his brother.
He replied: "It's too bad.
But I can't feel too sad.
After all I still have myself and my mother."

--

In Edmonton there's a population boom.
Construction is on the way to make more room,
Population has reached 877.926 people.
And there are more churches with a steeple.
Watch! Edmonton will be larger than Calgary zoo.

--

In Carman, Manitoba, the name of a postman is Harry.
Every letter delivered he was merry.
One day, however, while at the post office he ate a plum.
And his breath smelled of rum.
And then, tried to date my friend Cherry, the Canary.

In the New Brunswick city of Saint John.
Kent first read the gospel of Saint John.
Before heading for his real estate examination.
Then went to his father for an explanation.
Kent eventually became successful realtor with his friend Johan.
--

In the Ontario city of Brampton lived realtor Kay Nora.
Whose hobby was fauna and flora.
She had and old age pension.
That led to a tension.
So she changed her name to Senorita Laura.
--

During the Calgary Stampede a young cowboy name Keith.
Got bucked off a horse and lost his teeth.
His friends said he was plucky.
And he himself said that he was lucky.
He did not need a funeral wreath.
--

In the Manitoba town of Steinbach, on the way to pick up his mail.
To protect himself from hail.
Ed hid behind a hay bail.
Where also hiding he met a friend recently released from jail.
Both got freighted when on a scale they saw a large snail.

--

In the British Columbia town of Peachland, Rick Sand has an interesting dog, an Alsatian.
When he bought him at the Pet Store, the dog had a reputation.
One day the dog went wild.
And bit a small child.
Without any justification.

--

In the Alberta hamlet of La Corey.
Janis Korry felt sad and sorry.
So she bought a pet.
Who she had to take to a vet.
Whose first name was Orry.

--

In Ottawa an artist by the name of Saint.
Swallowed several samples of paint.
All shades of the spectrum.
Flowed out of his rectum.
With a colourful lack of restraint.
--

Victoria artist Jane with her canvas and stand.
Has a pallet and a paint brush in her hand.
She paints what she sees.
And like Emily Carr paints a landscape with trees.
The sea, the shore and the sand.
--

A young Toronto yuppie named Paul.
Was having a ball.
With good-looking Yvonne.
Partying until dawn.
In the end, remembering nothing at all.
--

Once Gaston visited France.
And learned how to do the vibrant cancan dance.
He twirled.
And swirled.
Until he lost his pants.
--

In the Saskatchewan town of Melville, there was a boy with a name Rick.
But his behaviour did not always tick.
He loved to get into a fist fight,
Even though he was very bright.
Once he got knocked out, he learned a lesson that one should always be quick.

--

In the British Columbia city of Trail, there was a farting contest in the smelting town.
Contestants came from miles around.
The first fart was extremely loud.
The second fart pleased the crowd.
After the third fart, the judge cried, "He shit his pants. Therefore the contestant is disqualified! What a clown!"

--

In the Alberta First Nation reserve of Hobbema there is a state of crises.
A crime wave that is similar to that operating in northern Iraq by ISIS.
In the four reserves that comprise the town,
All residents frown.
 The war-like gangs who drive-by and shoot people without a gun license.

--

In Hamilton there was a young man, Stan, who loves the game of football.
He was waiting for the CFL to call.
And while drinking beer and watching games on TV.
Between you and me.
Because of his drinking he soon was unable to crawl.

--

In the Saskatchewan town of Estevan, lived a guy named Van.
Who with his wife did the cancan.
Later each had a terrible stomach ache so they sat on a chair.
Saying, "It's only fair.
Because we each ate the entire chocolate cake", and then ran.

--

In the Ontario city of Thunder Bay there was a boy named Matt.
Who during a church sermon brought in a ball and a bat.
When asked why?
He would reply.
"Because I'm anxious to show off my new Blue Jays hat.``

--

In the Alberta town of Rocky Mountain House.
Henry was always afraid of a mouse.
He thought it was neat.
Not to treat.
The mouse like he had once treated a louse.
--
In the Alberta community of Holyoke.
The reason why children go to school is not to joke.
But to learn an important rule.
Anyone can be a fool.
And while having dinner not to choke.
--
Near the Alberta resort of Alder Flats, stats showed although she wasn't dumb.
While at school Cindy enjoyed wearing different hats and chewing bubble gum.
She would eat a crumb.
Beat a drum.
And then meet her chewing chum.
--

In the Alberta community of Czar.
Which is kind of far.
After committing perjury.
Dominic had surgery.
Leaving him with a huge scar.
--
In the Alberta town of Beaverlodge.
Lived a young lady named Mable Hodge.
While in the bath salts, one day.
In the tub where she lay.
Turned out to be a piece of hodgepodge.
--
Annabelle has developed lot of confidence over the years.
She has lost her fears.
Not afraid of mule deer's.
Doesn't believe in everything she hears.
Seldom dose one see her in tears.
--
The door to door election campaign was a disaster.
Some say one should come faster.
No matter how you vote: Conservative, Liberal or NDP.
Everyone is anxious to see.
If Prime Minster Harper will still be the Master.

There`s nothing like having a nap in the afternoon.
For an individual, a racoon or a baboon.
And if one isn't immune to be a buffoon.
It's an ideal time to draw a cartoon or take a ride in an air balloon.
With any whom.
--
In Major League Baseball, the Toronto Blue Jays.
Were playing the Tampa Bay Rays.
Jose Bautista was having fun.
After he hit another home run.
The Blue Jays win in so many ways.
--
In Major League Baseball, the Toronto Blue Jays were playing the Detroit Tigers.
A team in the American League known as a team of fighters.
Toronto starting pitcher, knuckleballer, R. A. Dicky, pitched a no hitter.
This made the Tigers bitter.
And so were the Detroit sports writers.
--

Toronto Blue Jays had a popular third baseman named Brett Lawrie.
Who because of injuries said he was sorry.
And traded to the Oakland Athletics for Josh Donaldson.
That was able to hit a home run.
And that's the Lawrie/Donaldson trade story
--
Blue Jay pitcher Drew Hutchison pitched a sinker.
But it became a stinker.
Then he threw a curve ball,
But it didn't curve an all.
Because at the time Drew was a blinker.
--
Edmonton Eskimo quarterback Matt Nichols.
Before a CFL game enjoyed a meal of pickles.
One day in a game against the Calgary Stampeders, he felt fickle.
So he gave himself a tickle.
The number of touchdowns he threw that day was one more than Brent Bickles.
--

Edmonton Eskimo quarterback Mike Reilly.
Visited the Alberta town of Riley.
After he had an accidental injury that was a dinger.
When he broke his finger.
That was taken care by Doctor Wiley.
--
The Edmonton Oilers.
Are a hockey team made up of toilers.
In order to make the NHL playoffs the team has to play tough.
But not too rough.
And the club would likely then become a team of playoff spoilers.
--
The Edmonton Oilers, recently a hockey team of losers and all I have to say.
Is how come the team cannot play as it used to during its heday?
And other NHL teams the Oilers used to blow away.
And the Stanley Cup in Edmonton would stay.
On display every day.
--

The Calgary based Pembina has made several pipeline deals.
And it has nothing to do with wheels.
It's to import methane.
And export propane.
As soon as the company finds its registry seals.
--
In the British Columbia town of Mission, there once lived a monk.
Who all of sudden was sprayed by a skunk.
So he jumped into the Fraser River where he found some dunk.
It wasn't funk.
But filth put in by a punk.
--
There was a young man named Sid in British Columbia's town of Sydney.
Who decided to donate a kidney.
That his close friend Mindy was in need.
And since he was a rare breed.
They both now call themselves Sid and Mindy.
--

A home is a roof to keep out the rain.
A place of refuge when one is in pain.
A home is residence where joy is shared
And nothing is spared.
Throughout the world, including Spain.
--

A Windsor, Ontario realtor named Ed was wise.
When he sold a high-rise.
A structure where one could touch the stars above the sky.
And tickle their feet as angels fly by.
Ed could sell, oh, how he could sell, even with his closed eyes.
--

The other day I was at the Winnipeg zoo.
Because I had nothing to do.
The tiger was there.
And so was the bear.
A lion, an elephant and several monkeys too.
--

A World News Report --
Russian president Vladimir Putin has bamboozled the West.
And not given it a rest.
First he invaded Crimea.
And tried the Ukraine while he had diarrhea.
What next? Putin said, "Put me to the test as I want to annex only the best."
--
Doggie doors eliminate middle man.
Please get me a door as quickly as you can.
Let my dog hit the yard without the need of a human gate keeper.
Even if my puppy is a sneaker.
And presently using a drip pan.
--
Young Rolfe.
 Was rough.
And tough.
While chewing his snuff.
And other stuff.
--

In Saskatchewan there's a community named Central Butte.
And girls are really cute.
Some play the guitar and some the flute.
And their music sounds toot-toot.
As they enjoy eating oranges and other fruit.

--

An Alberta man in the town of Clyde.
During a funeral procession was spied.
When asked, "Who is dead?"
He smiled and said:
"I don't know. I just came for the ride.

--

In the Newfoundland-Labrador town of Churchill Falls, 80-year old Alvin Hearst saw a coffin in a hearse.
And said, "For me this could be worse.
Of course the expense.
Is simply immense.
I'm delighted however; because I have insurance, it won't come from my purse."

--

It was building an object.
A build –at- home project.
However, it had a subject.
That I didn`t object.
If the judges find a defect.

I`m old enough to remember:
When Lester was born in September.
Nineteen years later, he was a UA student during an October.
Got married to Jocelyne and with her, helped Santa during December.
Its moments like this I shall remember for ever.
--
Here's a news item of the Week.
In Canada there was a handsome Greek.
Who English he did not speak.
As an immigrant he also could not French speak.
He could a bit, after taking lessons last week.
--
Earl McCain.
Had a strange flash come across his brain.
It happened while he was on a CNR train.
This might sound insane.
It happened while there was no rain.
--

Former Edmonton mayor Stephen Mandel
inspired us all.
Not to fall.
Behind in paying our annual taxes.
Even if you at one time lived in Texas.
In order not to pay a late fine, you can pay it at City Hall.

--

Edmonton firefighter called Fearless Fred.
Has a problem each morning while getting out of bed.
At the time he must rise.
He cannot open his eyes.
His entire body feels like a tonne of lead.

--

As fireman Fred reeled in his hose.
In Edmonton it was so cold that he almost froze.
Unless he got some heat.
From his head to his feet.
His body soon would decompose.

--

On my grandma's farm.
There's lot of charm.
The roosters crowed.
Even when it snowed.
And the coyotes did no harm.

Eating goober peas.
With limburger cheese.
Is a treat.
For one to eat.
Peas/cheese with anything else they please.
--
Schneider.
The lively spider.
Has 8 legs and 2 fangs.
And hangs.
On his web to catch a female insect and hide her.
--
Farmer John has a cow.
Chickens and a sow.
Plus a dog that barks, "Bow-Wow",
A cat that says, "Meow-Meow".
And a turkey that says, "Gobble-gobble, How-how?"
--

On John's farm hay, potatoes and wheat did grow.
Because of the inclement weather they grew slow.
At this time John had no agricultural products to show.
Potatoes to hoe.
Or hay to mow.
--
Jake rhymed a filthy nursery rhyme.
Of a derogatory kind.
The next time.
He tried one more time.
This time he composed a popular rhyme.
Of a different kind.
--
We sang 'Jingle Bells' in a two horse sleigh.
To a school concert two miles away.
On our way back home we watched the northern lights.
And in the distance Air Canada flights.
Directed by AMA.
--

Frosty, the Snowman.
In Afghanistan.
First sat on an oilcan.
And then across the border he ran.
To Iran.

--

Teacher Fred McCoy.
One day in his class room said to each girl and boy.
"Come and pick up your favorite toy.
Guaranteed to employ.
A lasting joy."

--

There was a grasshopper that had issue with an ant.
And wanted to take issue with a snail but it said, "I can't"
Then a mosquito came with a rant.
Followed by a spider who has a web on a bush plant.
Caught the grasshopper in its web and then sang a chant.

--

Hinky Dinky.
Was a friend with Pinkie Winkie.
But Pinkie was stinky.
And Dinky felt wimpy.
And the four were skimpy.
--
If you are happy, everyone will know it.
So stay happy and don't blow it.
Eat an apple a day
That will make feel okay.
Is one way to be happy and show it.
--
Each Sunday.
Mother makes me an ice cream sundae.
She makes me eat a banana each Monday.
And an Oreo cookie each Tuesday.
And fish on Friday.
--
While I was singing a song.
My friend Peter Wong came along
And we went to Century Park.
When it began to rain and getting dark
By going to the park, I think, I was wrong.
--

Shoe repairman Maurice repairs my shoes.
A trade he didn't want to choose.
When told as a lad.
That he must follow his dad.
He agreed in case his father blew a fuse.
--
In the British Columbia town of Fort Nelson,
there was a young man named Wilson Dar.
Who while enjoying a Cuban cigar.
Paid for his second-hand car.
Pulled on the choke.
And left the used car lot in a cloud of smoke that drifted far.
--
First there was fascism.
Then communism.
And now terrorism.
Extra-terrestrial and skepticism.
All we need now is more heroism.
--
How many birds are there in a flock?
It depends on the clock.
How many bees are there in a hive?
It depends dead or alive.
If one knew the answer it would be a shock.
--

In the Nova Scotia town of Pictou,
Christopher Bernard.
Is a bard.
Who with regard.
Uses his credit card.
As he has worked very hard.
--
While I was in British Columbia's village of McBride I was about to go to Moe's.
To see two of his shows.
However, a problem arose.
When I got a bloody nose.
Sometimes, that's the way it goes.
--
Near Brandon, Manitoba while on a train.
A Zombie approached me and wanted my brain.
He had already approached a Winnipeg chick.
That was built like a brick.
Zombies don't eat anyone who is plain or a passenger on an Air Canada plane.
In the Nova Scotia town of Truro, there's a vampire named Mable.
Whose periods come regular and stable.
Every full moon.
During the month of June.
She drinks herself under the table.

My brain turns to ice.
Every time I see mice.
Doing all sorts of household tricks.
Which are more difficult to fix
Than getting rid of head lice.
--

In the town of Banff each spring.
When robin feathers preen as they sing.
The birds don't know the actual date.
Except it's time to find a mate.
And time for another fling.
--

In Saskatchewan's Meadow Creek.
While we were playing hide-and-seek.
The weather was unique.
My friend Donald called it, "Bleak."
So I and Don ran to a shelter for comfort to seek.
--

Row, row, row your boat
To the nearest island you will float.
Where you will meet pretty Sandra Bolt.
Waiting for you to elope.
As soon as you kiss her throat.
--

In the Colombian capital of Bogota.
Lived two men by the name of Alah.
And Anois, his brother-in law.
Both made their living by exporting coffee beans to Canada.
When asked about their exports one replied,
"Oh. Why don't you first ask Lady Gaga"
--
In the Alberta town of Grande Cache.
Frank Ash had a large mustache.
As he was short of cash.
While driving to a bank and eating hash,
In a flash he had his car crash.
--
Theresa lives near Alberta's Moose Lake.
At eight she first learned how to skate.
At 18 a mate showed her how to bake.
And as time would dictate she traveled to Kuwait.
And since then is traveling around the world to prove she isn't a fake
--

Anita Trudeau lives in a Baie-Comeau, Quebec chateau.
And knows something about B. O.
In buying a deodorant however, she is slow.
Saying to herself, "I' in status quo. Easy come. Easy go.
I better tallyho."

--

Instead of a conventional marriage.
Let's meet in a carriage.
And once we make contact.
We'll sign a fixed term contract.
As part of our heritage.

--

In Cornwall, Ontario while sitting on a stool.
I met a lady serenading a mule.
Her name is Reese.
And she is obese.
And behaved like a fool.

--

It's the loveliest night of the year.
And I have no fear.
Because we have confirmed that it's true.
"I love you.
You are my love, my dear."

--

There are appropriate times to give flowers as a gift as they delight our senses.
During spring one can give a violet. During summer a rose while wearing sun glasses.
During autumn it's appropriate to give a heartsease (violet) flower.
During winter a holly is the favourite during a baby or wedding shower.
Flower can be delivered to most premises.
--
Vegetables are good eating during any season.
And for a good reason.
From January until December one can enjoy squash – broccoli – carrots – turnips - onions – celery – beats. and potatoes.
Also, lettuce – corn – beans – rhubarb – pumpkin – spinach and tomatoes,
During a pre or post season.
--
The truth is hard to beat.
During the summer heat.
And winter changed the world
When Earl became a tomboy girl
Now that the change made it complete
--

If you don't go.
You won't know.
The amount of snow.
In Buffalo.
Compared to a year ago.
--
While in Vancouver
Revi was driving a Rover,
He drove towards the sea.
Between you and me.
The setting sun he did not see.
--
In the New Brunswick city of Fredericton,
there was a lady named Mrs. Black,
Who had a sore back.
So her husband, Mack.
Gave her a whack.
And her health came back.
--
While sitting on a hutch.
I did Mable a favour so she said, "Thank you so much".
I said, "So much. How much is that?"
She didn't hear me so she said, "What?"
Her response I did not touch.
--

"Oh, what a technological thing will they think up next?"
Read a Joan to Jane cell phone text.
There is Google, Facebook LinkedIn, RSS Reader. Skype and Twitter.
YouTube, Pinterest, Instagram and a TV screen that is an inch thick or a bit thicker.
One wonders which of the above will be annexed.
--
1
I'll take the mop and you, Nancy, take the broom.
And we'll find ourselves in the laundry room.
Singing musharoom, musharoom, musharay,
Our love is here to stay.
All the way. Every day.
Boom. Boom. Boom. Boon!

2
I've seen Nancy smile and weep.
I've also seen her sleep.
After we each sang musharoom, musharoom, musharay.
Our love is here to stay.
Beep. Beep. Beep. Beep.

3
I also heard Nancy snore.
Not like before.
When we sang, musharoom. musharoom, musharay.
Our love is here not to stay.
Because of the loud snore I don't love her any.
More, More, More, More.
--
On the Arctic island of Alert.
Lives a lad by the name of Burt.
Whenever he sees a young female he begins to flirt.
By saying, "You are wearing a beautiful skirt.
I always thought you were a squirt."
--
In Scotland lived poet Robbie Burns.
Who aside poetry and songs had concerns.
About germs.
And the tune Auld Lang Syne, Scotch whiskey, baggase.
And haggis and the small amount of money a poet earns.
--

My husband Ned is great - good as gold.
Even though he is a bit old.
He loves me a lot.
Especially when I'm hot.
And after an investment he has sold.
--
In the Saskatchewan town of Aberdeen lives a bachelor by the name of Gord O'toole.
Who found red spots on his tool.
His doctor was a cynic,
Said, "Get out of this clinic.
Don't drule. You fool."
--
In the Ontario city of Sarnia, there is a dog.
Who is in love and has started a blog.
He reports the news.
With barking reviews.
Then because of success he celebrates with eggnog.
--
In the B, C, village of New Denver there was a schnauzer named Pete.
Eye-browed and so neat.
He wanted to win.
But failed to begin.
For the bitch had gone into heat.
--

The wine my ancestor's drank.
I found in an old copper tank.
It was bitter and red.
And went straight to my head.
As into a stupor I sank.
--
A fan can win $50 and more.
If 2 punts are returned and score.
As you probably know.
Safeway is offering a million, to any Joe.
And if you don't win, don't feel sore.
--
Wendy and Tom own two cats.
And these are the facts.
One is named Pussy and the other Kitty.
Both are pretty.
Although they have spats while chasing rats.
--
There once were 2 cats in the town of Benny,
Who each thought there was one cat to many
They scratched and they bit.
The fought and they spit.
Till instead of two cats, there weren't any.
--

In Ontario's Kingston city.
Lorraine had a cute kitty.
Who thought it might.
Get thrown out at night.
If it did, what a pity.

--

In Plum Coulee, Manitoba, there's a mice infestation.
Greatest in the entire nation.
If there is one?
There most likely are thirty-one.
And no cats, even after an invitation.

--

Charlie Spratt lives in an Edmonton flat
Which he shares with skinny Kitty Cat.
At the moment Charlie isn't here.
Hasn't been seen for a year.
Kitty has grown extremely lazy and fat.

--

A dog, cat and a flea.
Sat down at Tim Horton's for a cup of tea,
They also ate some ham.
With bread and jam.
And were content as can be.

--

In Edmonton there's a cat crises at the Humane Society.
The number of stray cats has reached 90.
The population is at maximum capacity.
Overcrowding with audacity.
From all parts of the city.
--
130 cats, 3 liter boxes were discovered in a home in Cox Cove, Newfoundland.
And Janis Higgins of Cat Rescue had difficulty to understand.
Why the cats were undernourished and suffering flea infestation.
Following an investigation.
To get rid of the stench, Janis needed volunteers to give her a hand.
--
Another stray cat came to our house.
Chasing a mouse.
Having caught it, it then attacked a grouse
So I said to my spouse:
If again I see a cat chasing a mouse, that's when I'll enjoy a
Pizza and sauce.
--

Gingerbread cats.
Dressed in whipped-cream hats.
Danced in a garden under a full moon.
To the rhythm of a wooden spoon.
Until came a pack of rats.

--

In Nepawin, Saskatchewan, Merle.
Has a dog named Chewy that will not chase a squirrel
And is allergic to cats.
Mice and rats.
And during winter wears furry apparel.

--

If cats could talk. What would they say?
Aside from 'meow, meow' they would say
words that will take your breath away.
When the sun shines from the East.
They would say: "It's time for a feast.
Catch a mouse and have a heyday."

--

Here are tips on refreshing old furniture.
Don't splurge, start slowly and take care when repairing the chair.
Ensure the furniture is sound no matter if it's round or square.
Don't make every piece to look alike when you repair the chair.
And remember you are repairing the furniture for now and the future.

--

University students beware!
There is something new in the air.
Your tuition fees will again increase.
Which never seem to cease.
And the government seems not to care.

--

Education.
Is an illumination.
 For any location.
In the entire nation.
Try and get it without hesitation.

--

A young Moncton, New Brunswick female teacher of a boy's class.
Took favours to allow them to pass,
Her husband was away.
And came home one day.
And kicked the boy's ass.
--
In a private Kamloops school.
During summer they dress sexy to keep cool.
You can believe me or not.
This makes the boys hot.
Which is against a school rule.
--
Jana Burke is a translator.
Who at one time lived near the Equator.
One day she was asked," Do you know how to translate Esperanto?"
"She said, "Sorry that's one language I do not know and must go.``
Straight to my defibrillator."
--

There was an engineering student named Troy.
At the University of Toronto be became a playboy.
His results at term end.
Lost him many a friend.
So he changed from being wild to being a choir boy.
--

In Victoria octogenarian Eva Niro
Moved in from Cairo
At age 85 a birthday cake
She did bake.
For her a Hungarian by the name of Laszlo Biro.
--

On Highway # 43, near Grande Prairie.
While driving, Mike Dee urgently wanted to poo and pee.
So in heavy traffic he stopped and by his car, let his pants down, and did his thing,
 Until the unusual incident did bring.
A cop and Mike was charged with obscenity.
--

Sir John Franklin was British explorer every day.
He disappeared on his expedition attempting to chart and navigate a section of the Northwest Passage in the Canadian Arctic on a payday.
Two icebound ships were abandoned.
And the entire 128 crew perished from starvation including member Ed.
The good news is that after 168 years and forty searches, one of the ships, Erebus, was found last Thursday.

--

American warship Reuben James during world war 11.
Was sunk in 1941 by the Germans and only a handful had a clue.
Of the 159-man crew only 44 survived.
The remaining had died.
Since then American military strategy came under a review.

--

Uncle Dominic Remus.
Has been asking for directions to Planet Venus.
It's a long distance away.
And says: "I would like to leave today.
On the rocket ship To Venus R us.``
--
In the British Columbia town of Surry.
Lived a young lady who was always in a hurry.
She called her husband a fool.
And drove her children to school.
Then had a pizza and sat on a stool that was furry.
--
In Kamloops, British Columba, Steven was a nervous young teacher.
Who taught his biology class like a preacher.
The pupil delight.
Was to put up a fight.
So they could not be removed from the bleacher.
--

Sue flunked her math test and felt blue.
Geometry she just could not do.
Algebra was easy.
Other subjects were breezy.
Sadly off the honor roll, Sue flew.

--

Category: Jewish Song Writers:--
Irving Berlin, Leonard Cohen, Mel Brooks, Mel Torme, Milton Ager
Burt Bacharach, Oscar Hammerstein 11. Marshal Barer
Richard Rodgers, Andrew Previn, Larry Rose. Steve Lieberman
Barry Manalo, Barbara Streisand, Victor Young, David Friedman
Barry Goldberg, George Cohan. Jay Livingston, Michael Masser

--

In Norman Wells, NWT Alex Monroe had 70 miles to go and as there was drifting snow.
He was driving slow.
When suddenly at Bear Creek 2 bears chased him up a spruce tree, shook and shook and nothing happened.
The 2 bears disappeared and minutes later 1 returned accompanied with a beaver, saddened.
While the beaver was cutting the tree down, Mr. Monroe let go and fell to the ground.
And kayoed the bear and the beaver with 2 blows in a row.
--
Brett is a Carman, Manitoba, plumber.
Who at the end of summer.
Wanted to hold a harvest fair.
But people didn't care.
So he bought himself a luxury Hummer.
--
In Guelph, Ontario lives 16-year old Joyce.
With a beautiful voice.
Under a light.
During the night.
Sings songs to rejoice.
--

The British Columbia town of Osoyoos is Canada's Arizona.
 And the home town of Felix and Ramona.
Its wine country and Osoyoos Lake has an amazing sandy beach.
Which is easy to reach.
Much easier than in Barcelona.
--
True to his profit and pride.
A Halifax millionaire has died.
At the funeral the wife was in tears.
Each time his name she hears
And runs to her bedroom to hide
--
When I'm not feeling well, I ask my daughter.
For a glass of water.
If I have high blood pressure with a friend of mine.
I enjoy a glass of wine.
If I'm still not feeling well, I'd call Alberta Health Care and hope my health doesn't falter.
--

There was a lady dancer by the name of Ann Chan.
Who lived in Japan.
And could dance the vibrant French cancan.
Then she moved to Kazakhstan and her partner was Diane.
And later to Spokane where she danced with Roseanne.
--
In Edmonton Ed was stuck in a long traffic jam.
As a protester approached his car and said he gave a damn.
Because the Alberta government severe austerity budget, Premier Allison Redford has been kidnaped and to be set on fire so the protesters are not asking a ransom but a donation.
So Ed asked, "What equation do you use from a corporation?"
The protester said, "About a gallon of gas per car and a slice of ham."
--

In Calgary a vicious snow storm left 30, 000 homes in the dark.
There were broken trees, traffic snarls and damage to the Princes Island Park.
It took several weeks to restore power outages and Mother Nature's destruction.
All went well again after a period of reconstruction.
The city crew worked day and night to give Calgary a bit of a spark.

--

A young Yellowknife realtor named Phips.
Got married while on one of his Northwest Territories trips.
It was a widow named Jane Block.
The realtor then nearly died of shock.
When he discovered there also were 2 little chips.

--

Rob Ford has withdrawn from the Toronto Mayoralty race.
Brother Doug took his place.
Rob however, will seek a council seat in word two.
And replace Mike, his nephew.
Most Torontonians say, "We need a change in direction and no longer Fords' to face.

Dan Danburger.
Is a Winnipeg factory worker.
While driving on the Trans-Canada Highway was enjoying a hamburger.
Stopped by a cop he could not driver further.
As he was charged with erratic driving that could possibly cause a murder.

--

Our generation.
Needs inspiration.
That of former Prime minister Pearson.
As one reason.
To continue Canada's future destination.

--

In Canada's Northwest Territory.
I had heard words that are inflammatory.
About Yellowknife, Tuktoyaktuk, Inuvik and Pine Point.
These communities were often called, 'Just a Joint'.
And residents living there are sorry.

--

One can cuddle me,
For a fee.
On land or the sea.
Between you and me.
Cuddling now isn't like it used to be.

Dennis Bork.
Is a Maritime Muslim that doesn't eat pork.
No matter if he's in Mecca or New York.
Until one day he met a long-billed stork.
Reminding Dennis he could eat anything he wants so long as he used a fork.

--

It was getting dark.
When Ivan was in a park.
And bitten by a flee
And then a bumble bee.
On his way home he heard a coyote bark.

--

Some say in Canada during winter there is lot of snow.
And there is nowhere to go.
Others say: "No. no. no.
Look at Joe.
He goes skating, tobogganing and hockey games even if its thirty below."

--

Felicity.
Lives in a city.
However, it's a pity.
She has lost her kitty.
That was pretty.

--

In God we should trust.
Otherwise our dreams could bust.
And left to rust.
If we are unjust.
And turn to dust.
--
My father Hugh.
Built a bicycle for two.
To be used by me and you.
Brother Lou.
And sister Sue.
--
Jimmy Lee.
The sailor, went to see.
The Mediterranean Sea.
On an Air Canada flight for free.
His journey ended. however, when Jimmy fell down and harmed his knee.
--
During a Wawa, Ontario Annual Bird Fair.
There were hundreds of species there.
Some with feathers, Some with hair.
Several holding a sign that read: "Look out for the bear.
Don't make us extinct. Take Care."
--

Environmentalist Henry Benz.
Suggests: Be kind to you web footed friends.
Especially that facilitate swimming.
And don't need screening.
Your comments this Friday ends.

--

Wilfred Pancky.
Is a Yankee.
Each month composes a Hanky-Panky song.
That in composition is sometimes wrong.
Even when he uses his hanky.

--

Down by the riverside.
On the north side.
Is a cottage that is safe and wide.
An ideal place to hide
During you honeymoon for you and your bride to hide.

--

Ike wanted to be a sportscaster.
Mike a newscaster.
Frank a war correspondent.
While in Afghanistan Frank became despondent.
And because of the dangerous insurgents, wished he could run faster.

--

Roy is a Toronto auctioneer.
Who holds auction sales far and near.
He suffers from diabetes and high blood pressure.
And the profit made at times he cannot treasure.
Roy is still making sales. He has no fear.

--

In Toronto there there's a notable family named Stein.
There's Gertrude, Ep and Ein.
Gertrude's prose is bunk.
Ep's sculpture is junk.
And no one understands Ein because she's helping others to brew moonshine.

--

Nova Scotia has put a temporary moratorium on oil and natural gas hydraulic fracturing as a resource.
The process is used where millions of gallons of water, sand and chemicals are piped underground to break the apart the rock and release the gas as recommended by an energy source.
Some scientists are worried that fracturing causes an earthquake.
While others say the theory is a mistake.
And to find natural gas by fracturing is better than using a horse.

--

Newfoundland-Labrador alcohol addict Dale has to remain in jail.
Because he has no money for the bail.
After he was involved in a fist fight.
And a foreigner broke his nose with a vicious right.
A cell cop says it's a sad tale and that Dale, can pay the fine in braille.

--

One can`t judge a book by its cover.
And if Jerry Glover or his brother is a lover.
All that glitters is not gold.
If Jerry is young or old.
We have to wait until his life span is over.
--

An Audubon Society report says that some birds are threatened by climate change.
The birds range:
From gannets, bald eagles, mallard ducks and the loon.
And the extinction could take place soon.
Several scientists however, say the report is a bit strange.
--

Here are the **morning** news headlines --
Scotland says "No" to become Independent.
In B.C, teachers strike ends, that was splendent.
Museum of Humanity opens in Winnipeg.
At the official opening, a protester is hospitalized after having whiskey swig.
A friend of his becomes a defendant.
--

Here are the latest **noon** news headlines --
UK PM thanks Scotland for voting No.
And says Scotland has room to grow.
Scottish National leader Alex Salmond, to resign.
And says defeat is a bad sign.
And voting yes was a big No, No.
--

Here are the latest **evening** news headlines --
Foreign secretary Baird speaks at the UN.
Burger King says take over Tim Horton's as soon as it can.
Ukraine thanks Canada for its help.
During a massive hurricane in Mexico, Canadian tourists are stranded and scream, `Yelp!
West Jet please get us out of here as quickly as you can!"
--

Here are the latest **Sports** headlines --
NFL Commissioner Roger Goodel, apologises for the latest football family and children abuse.
Texas Ranger Manager Ron Washington, after divorcing his wife says ``What's the use?"
--

Edmonton Oilers begin training for the 1914-1915 hockey season.
Toronto Blue Jays do not make the AL playoffs and fans wonder what's the reason?
In the CFL the Ottawa Redblacks in order to win, will have to elevate by drinking more apple juice.

--

The latest **weather** forecast for Toronto -- Forecaster Heather says:
"Lots of snow after going through a drought. The wind is 100 kilometers per hour or there about.
And following a flood one can shout:
"Next year due to a climate change, we hope we have better days."

--

While on my way home from school.
I met a weirdo who at one time lived in Istanbul.
He had bleary eyes.
And was about 6 feet tall in size.
After a brief conversation, I discovered the stranger was a cool fool.

--

3:30 and school is out.
Students are running about.
There is notoriety and the elite.
With the teachers do not wish to meet.
There is pandemonium throughout.
--
In Canada the rich get richer.
And the poor get poorer.
Those in the middle get squeezed.
As if breezed.
And remain bitter.
--
I needed a front door for my hall.
The replacement I bought was too tall.
So I hacked it and chopped it.
And carefully lopped it.
And now the dumb thing is too small.
--
In the British Columbia town of Smithers.
A bank teller got the dithers.
When a stranger from Beirut.
Held up a bank in a yellow suit.
And to a teller said, "Hand me the money and I don't care if you have the shivers``
--

There was a lady in Berlin.
Who was excessively thin.
She had no fear.
To drink Canadian beer.
Some Germans thought she was committing a sin.
--
On Canada's East Coast.
Once lived a ghost.
Who first was a stocker.
And then became a door knocker.
Near midnight, the ghost was feared the most.
--
When I was in love.
I met a dove.
Who came along.
And we sang a song.
As Angels watched from above.
--
A lady from the South African city of Pretoria.
Came to visit a friend in British Columbia`s Victoria.
They danced, dined and wined.
Their friendship soon shined.
And became a state of euphoria.
--

In Halifax, Max had a bad day.
When he was on the way.
His computer crashed.
Car tires were slashed.
Worse of all, his wallet was stolen during mid-day.
--
In Edmonton, John had a bad day.
During the month of May.
After a long day at work he was tired.
His love life wasn't inspired.
And he had lost his pay.
--
In Vancouver, Bill Hoover had a bad day.
After he lost his pay.
Had to borrow from Visa to pay Master Charge.
So he could pay for a barge.
Till then he had nowhere to stay.
--
In Montreal, Pierre had a bad day.
Along with wife Kay.
Got a speeding ticket.
Nearly ran down a striking picket.
And wasn't allowed inside a certain café.
--

In Victoria, there was a retired man who averred
And learned to fly like a bird.
Cheered by 100 people.
He leaped from a church steeple.
Statistics were kept when this occurred.
--
In the Alberta hamlet of Calahoo.
Lived Lou, who I knew.
He had a large wart on his nose which was removed.
His appearance improved
As soon as he found the bird cuckoo.
--
Everybody is an insider.
As the program of distinction becomes wider and wider.
No member can become a hider.
Even a whistle blower who is beside her.
Or a cowboy who is a Calgary Stampede rider.
--

In the Manitoba town of Carberry, Ray to Mae had his final say.
When Ray said, "Our relationship ends today.
I wish you the best.
With your holiday zest.
It's my turn to go out and play."
--
In the New Brunswick town of Campbellton, Brick.
A local hick.
Called a chic lady with a stick,
 A **chick.**
This struck me as sexist and made me sick.
--
Oh, what have I done with my resume list?
Of foreign workers who want to work in Canada to exist.
Resumes from India, Morocco and Spain.
Philippines, China, and Ukraine.
And there are other countries which I may have missed.
--

There are some, who are averse.
To my limerick verse.
In their emails, they perverse.
And of course, some curse.
And I don't know which is worse – writing heroic limerick verse or being married to an angry divorced scrub nurse?
--
Vatican!
Vatican!
"Come to Rome to discuss issues confronting the Catholic Church."
Pope Francis instructed 200 world bishops to discuss where the present faith controversies lurch.
And said: "Let's awaken and take a fresh look at our gay, divorce and remarriages policy quickly as we can.
--
In Nova Scotia's Annapolis Valley Ms. Kelly likes to lie in the sun,
Absorbing those rays just for fun.
One day while enjoying a bologna bun.
That weighed almost a metric ton.
Ms. Kelly with a full belly wasn`t able to run.
--

Torontonians are polite.
Says a study and it is right.
While Montrealers try with all their might.
And even want to fight.
The city of Toronto is a wonderful sight,
especially at night.

--

There once was a Canadian senator named Jack Veep.
Who during senate meetings always fell asleep.
He even couldn't have a peep.
Or weep.
In the end Senator Veep by other senators was called a Creep.

--

A day for me that is unique like no other.
Isn't with my brother or father.
But a day when I bus traveled with my mother.
We were laughing and joking at each other.
Where at one point after hearing us, the bus driver stopped and said, "You are 2 goofy loonies and I can't driver any farther."

--

Yesterday I visited my Hoselaw, Alberta mother- in-law.
As she was wearing a hat made out of straw.
I was at awe as we talked about the past.
But she was talking so fast.
The visit I had to withdraw.

--

There was a young lady from the Luxembourg town of Wiltz.
Who traveled to Scotland and for walking used her stilts.
Relatives were embarrassed.
The lady was harassed.
The following day she wore her kilts."

--

Its Halloween night.
Pumpkin faces are aglow and there is a lot of fright.
Skeletons hang from the wall.
Witches and ghosts are on the crawl.
Regardless, it's an interesting Halloween fright sight.

--

During Halloween tricks and treats can upset pets.
One often forgets.
To keep the noise level down and close the doors.
So tricking doesn't harm their feeling remorse.
Playing smooth music is better than the pets hearing overhead flying jets.

--

I often print on the sand.
With my right hand.
The words I find difficult to say.
And hope the wind will send the message your way.
And you will find it grand. I hope you understand.

--

I can see it clear as day.
The local bird of prey.
In the battle of the sky.
That includes a blue jay attacked by a magpie.
Birds of prey include: the candor, eagle, falcon, vulture, hawk and more.
Victims usually are sore including: a starling, chicken, humming bird and a canary.

--

After the ashes are scattered from my urn.
If the Lord gave me another chance to return.
There is no doubt which bird I'd want to be.
A British Columbia eagle perched on a pine tree.
Presently a bird of extinction concern.
--
God told Noah to build an ark.
To make it out of cypress wood but no bark.
Noah did as was asked.
And worked until he completed his task.
He worked even if it was dark.
--
When it came for Noah's ark to depart.
The birds and animals came out 2 by 2
From the start.
In pairs they strolled off the ark.
The birds weren't far apart.
Getting off last was the lark.
--
When Noah brought the pairs to his arch.
Conditions nearby were stark.
Then from above.
Came a dove.
And showed Noah where to park.
--

Are you sure?
At night, walking down-town that you are secure.
Your ear muffs were made with fur.
You used marijuana as a cue.
Or stepped on a pile of manure.
--
Are you sure, sure?
You have helped the poor.
Your son, Napoleon, is mature.
Your family name is still Couture.
If you've been to Kuala Lumpur.
--
Are you sure, sure, sure?
That your husband is an entrepreneur.
In literature.
He is wealthy.
More than you ever were.
--
I'll find you rivers and stars.
A way to reach Mars.
A 9th Symphony that isn't cursed.
Conducted by Sidney Hearse.
And performed for the NHL All-Stars.
--

It was a lovely mystic night.
The full moon was shining bright.
The trees glistened under the moon.
As I walked singing a happy tune.
It was a lovely night to fly a kite.
--

Nights are long.
Summer days are gone.
Spring will soon come along.
And we can sing a song.
Accompanied with a gong.
--

Jane Seabit in Port McNeil, B. C, had a pet frog named Bibbit.
As she was heading for school it said, "Skip it".
Jane thought this was insane.
When the frog called her name,
Even though the frog was explicit.
--

 Cherry Sather. A Lake Ontario bather, whose clothing was strewed.
By winds that left her nude.
A handsome man came along,
And unless I'm wrong.
You expected this line to be lewd.
--

In our neighborhood is an owl named Boo.
Every night on a tree top it says, "Who, who."
One evening a young boy walked by.
And started to cry.
And replied, "I don't have clue."

--

Early in the morn.
I blow my trumpet horn.
The birds are still asleep.
The crickets do no peep.
And farmer Bjorn is already planting his corn

--

A bomb
With Tom
No wife
Sad life
Aplomb - keep calm

--

Be careful when climbing a ladder.
Climbing down you could be sadder.
Be kind to those you meet.
The same people you will greet.
And be careful of your urinary bladder.

--

The saddest eyes I had ever seen in Gloria were green.
Because of broken promises and a broken dream.
Looking closely at her eyes I could see.
Between you and me.
That Gloria's life of unhappiness had been.
--
Phoebe.
Is a young lady with a saying of if and maybe.
Seldom ready.
To go steady.
And says, "First I have to think it over and see."
 --
Mike Baik.
After someone stole his bike.
Went on strike.
First he went on a hike.
And overtook a killer mosquito bite.
--
Our personal war.
No more.
To even the score.
From before.
The arguments we had we should ignore.
--

Dorothy Cox.
Is smart as a fox.
She didn't wear any socks.
Until she fell in love with Bobby Knox.
Who taught her how to wrestle and box.
--
Have you ever been in court?
When as a traveller you lost your passport?"
As a last resort the judge said, "Have a snort.
 Put on your overcoat.
As it time for you to deport."
--
In the Alberta town of Onoway.
There was a lady visiting Canada from Norway.
Who sat in a doorway.
When the wind messed her hat.
She asked, "What is that?"
It's a strange way to celebrate my birthday."
--
There was a gent in Australia.
Who was in love with Dahlia.
Both were fine.
As they would dine
Near an azalea.
--

Sam from Beirut.
Women he did not give a hoot.
He would stand.
In a manner that was grand,
When a snake-charmer played on his flute.

--

Every day.
In every way.
Night or day.
Agnes Day.
Would say: "If you want to stay? It has to be my way.``

--

Dick.
Did a bad trick.
When he said to friend Nick, "If you are kind to me?
I will be kind to thee."
As it turned out Dick was a rural hick.

--

Niccolo Machiavelli.
Lived in a valley.
He was a 14th century Italian historian, politician, philosopher, humanist and a writer.
Compared to his contemporaries he seemed to be much brighter.
He wrote the masterpiece Prince which gained enormous notoriety.
From sobriety.
Because as an author Machiavelli endorsed behaviour that was evil, immoral and unpredictable like a jelly.
--
Ted Sorenson was President Kennedy's long-time advisor.
He was a lawyer and a legendary speech writer.
Sorenson is best known for Kennedy's speech **Ask Not**.
Which is thought of a lot.
And made America wiser.
--

Tenor Ben Heppner (1956 -) lived in B. C.s Dawson Creek.
His parents were relatively poor and the economy was week.
Ben however, entered the New York Opera Search for Talent Contest and won.
For the next 25 years he sang operates throughout the world and had fun.
Now retired and employed by the CBC as a radio broadcaster before leaving for work.
Ben gives wife a peck on her cheek
--
Emily Carr (1971-1945) was a Canadian artist and writer.
At the time no Canadian was mightier.
She was inspired by indigenous people of the Pacific Northwest coast and did a lot of fishing.
But did not receive widespread recognition.
As she studied in France and matured, the subject of her painting shifted from aboriginal themes to a forest landscape.
Born in Victoria, Emily was the second youngest of 9 and lived in the English tradition from summer to winter.
--

Canadian contralto singer Maureen Forester was born in Montreal.
And made her 1956 classical debut in the New York Town Hall.
Maureen performed regularly in concerts and opera abroad.
In her later life she suffered from dementia and loved God.
In Toronto she died in 2004 and described by news media as a `Wonderful Doll`.
--
Polish pianist Fredric Chopin (1810-1849) composed Polonaise when he was eight.
Without the help of his parents or a playmate.
He was born near Warsaw and at 20 left for France.
Where he had a better chance.
To play the piano and fans to dance.
--

Jean Beliveau (1931- 2014) was a Montreal Canadian great hockey hero for a 20 seasons
In that time he won 10 Stanley Cups and Canadians loved him for many other reasons
He was a legend on and off the ice
A person that was kind and nice
During a funeral thousands prayed that Beliveau enter heaven and stay there during all seasons.

--

Father Albert Lacombe (1827-1916) was an Alberta pioneer missionary.
His achievements with aboriginal people were extraordinary.
He brokered peace between the Cree and Blackfoot negotiating construction of the Canadian Pacific Railway through Blackfoot territory.
And that wasn't the only category.
He established a mission and was buried in Saint Albert near Edmonton. His many other achievements have become legendary.

--

The Alberta city of Leduc is named after the Very Reverend Father Hippolete Leduc. 91842-1928)
Who became a priest in Ottawa and while in Saint Albert near Edmonton, Indian Cree lessons he took.
In the year 1887 was the year Canada became a nation.
And Father Leduc spent most of his time with the Cree and became a sensation.
He died at age 76 and while speaking Cree there were several words he mistook.
--
Victor Borge (1909-2000) was a Danish classical pianist, entertainer and humorist.
And quickly became known as a music satirist.
He moved to America in1941 and became known as the Crown Prince of Denmark.
At his concerts it was usually difficult to find a place to park.
Borge made thousands of people laugh including many a monarch.
--

Archimedes (287 BC-212 BC was a famous mathematician and inventor in ancient Greece.
For his discovery as the principal of the Archimedes' screw was a masterpiece.
Archimedes died during the 2nd Punic war when Roman forces captured his city of Syracuse as for Archimedes they had no use.
After the war Planet Earth, due to the Archimedes invention, there was temporary peace.

--

John Jacob Astor (1763-1848) as a German born American businessman.
He was the first multi-millionaire in Untied States and not Japan.
After the fur trade declined he diversified by investing in New York real estate.
And found himself Sarah Cox Todd as a mate.
Later, Astor became a billionaire and became a famous patron of the arts.
Quickly as one can.

--

Orpheus was a legionary musician, poet and prophet in ancient Greece.
He could charm all living things and with his wife Eurydice, both lived in peace.
Orpheus was the greatest of all poets and musicians in the world.
Until his wife disappeared and his world unfurled.
Some in the underworld were jealous of Orpheus and killed him before he could see his new born niece.

--

Pauline Johnson (1861-1913) was a popular Canadian writer and performer in the late 19th century.
In Branford, Ontario of Mohawk and Dutch ancestry.
In 1909 she moved to Vancouver and enjoyed paddling a canoe near Stanley Park.
Through her writings and the poem - "The Song My Paddle Sings", she was in everyone's heart.
Pauline Johnson died of breast cancer in Vancouver and Canadians still hold her poems in their memory.

--

Dylan Thomas (1914-1953) was a Welsh poet who could write
His works include the poem: "Do not go gentle into the night."
Although Thomas as popular poet, was articulate.
He found making a living difficult.
He was an alcoholic and was found dead one night.
--
Cole Porter (1891-1964) was an American composer and song writer.
And also an all-nighter.
Born to a wealthy family in Indiana he defied wishes of his domineering grandfather and took up music as a profession.
Where in each individual session
Cole created songs like "I get a kick of You", "Night and Day"
And a series of Broadway,
Musicals like: Kiss Me Kate, Can-Can, Gay Divorcee and others that in structure were lighter.
--

Seventeen year-old Malala Yousatzai is a Pakistani activist for female education
In her Muslim nation.
Malala and Kailash Satyrthai of India bonded together and each became a Nobel Prize Laureate.
For their advocacy in not banning girls from attending school and started International Action
For the world to communicate to the Taliban reaction.
In a short while Malala became a Pakistani girl, for a girl like her to obtain an education.
Became a sensation.

--

Stephen Foster (1826-1864) was an American song composer.
During 1850 he met Jane McDowell and married her.
Foster wrote over 200 songs including Oh! Susana and Old Black Joe.
Old Folks at Home. Beautiful Dreamer and More Years to Go.
By 1860 Foster, like Dylan Thomas, was struggling with alcoholism and died in 1864 in a life closer.

--

James Naismith (1861-1939) was a Canadian/American Sports coach and innovator.
And also a basketball chaplain who had a degree as a doctor.
Naismith invented the sport game of basketball in 1891 and wrote the original rule book.
Which to the Canadian Sports and the Olympic hall of Fame he took.
No matter what the basketball score.
--
Wilf Carter also known as Montana Slim (1904-1096) was a Canadian cowboy.
Carter was born in Port Hilford, Nova Scotia and after falling out with his father who was Baptist minister, moved to Calgary while still a young boy.
Eventually Carter lived in United in United States and moved to Calgary and wrote hundreds of songs like: The Last Roundup, Blue Canadian Rockies and You Are My Sunshine. He appeared on both Canadian and American radio networks and was popular in Nashville.
Carter had two daughters Carol and Sheila who are entertainers still.

Carter was inducted into the Canadian and American Music hall of Fame and due to loss of hearing died in Arizona at the age of 91. Now Wilf Carter is recognized in Canada and United States as an inspirational and popular music yodeling cowboy.

--

Albert Johnson (?- 1931) also known as the Mad Animal Trapper of the Rat River Territory.

Johnson was a Canadian criminal whose history during the Great Depression made one worry.

And sparked a huge manhunt in the Northwest Territories and the Yukon in 1931. After Johnson had shot several policemen and eluded the RCMP for more than a month while he was on the run.

Johnson didn't have a mandatory trapping license and the local trappers complained that he had invaded their territory.

Eventually in -40F weather Johnson was shot and never apologised that he trapped illegally and was sorry.

--

The Wright Brothers (Orville (1871-1948) and Wilbur (1867-1912) were two American Brothers who invented the first airplane.
As soon aa they receive their patent in 1903 they enjoyed a glass of champagne.
Alexander graham Bell (1847-1922) a Canadian (Nova Scotia) is credited in1876 with inventing the first telephone.
And now one could communicate by phone, plane and train,
--
Women Inventors –
! -- Mary Anerson (1866-1953) invented the windshield wiper blade. Stephanie Kwoleek (1923-2014) invented the first known Klever, Florence Gave invented the Self-Cleaning-House termite prrof washer.
2 – Marion Donavan (1917-1998) invented the first disposable diaper, Marie Currie (1867-1934) a Polish chemist, discovered the elements of radium, Temple Grandin (1947 -) an autistic woman became an expert on animal behavior.

3 –Ruth Handler (1916-2002) in 1059 invented the Barbie Doll, Mary Phelps (1891-1970) invented the Modern Brassiere, Katherine Burr Crosby
(1898-1979) incented the non-reflective glass used in cameras, car windshields and computer screens, Valerie Thomas (1945-2009), an African American, in 1977 invented the illusion transmitter.

4 – Lydia Newman (1885 -?) An African American invented the modern hair brush, Margaret Knight (1838-1914) invented the Big Paper Machine, Ann Tsukamoto, is an American stem cell researcher.

5 – Ellen ochoa (1958 -) is the worlds first Hispanic Astronaut, Madame C. Walker *1867-1919) was an American entrepreneur and philanthropist to be the first American female to become a millionaire, Helen Walton (1919-2007) was the wife on Walmart founder Samuel Walton (1943-1992) at one point in her life was the the richest American and eleventh richest in the world. There was no one like her.
--

Buxton, Ontario is a settlement made up of African-American refugees.
Who arrived in Canada by means of an underground railroad in the 1840`s and 50`s.
They settled by the hundreds and because of their bravery.
In Canada found civil rights and freedom from slavery.
A historic site museum includes a residence and a barn that brings memories to whoever the museum sees.

--

There will always be a Canada, red white and the male leaf.
Strong, free and seldom in grief.
If Canada means as much to me and you.
An what other countries say is true.
The democratically- elected Prime Minister will always be the Chief.

--

The Indian Ocean 9.1 earthquake and tsunami took place in 2004.
It was an Asian calamity that did not happen before.
It was one of the deadliest natural disasters in history.
And still a mystery.
Why Indonesia was the hardest hit and 230,000 people, including 16 Canadians were killed and relatives remain sore.
--
Doctors Without Borders.
Do not take appointment orders.
They are an international group that treat people where the need is the greatest.
The Ebola disease epidemic outbreak in West Africa is the latest.
Where the doctors have become tired workers.
--
Keep the Home Fires burning (Till the Boys Come Home) is a World War 1 song.
It became popular in the United Kingdom and Canada. And then came along.
'It's a Long Way to Tipperary'.
This made the home people cheerful and merry.
When the war was over and gone.

The 7 deadly sins are:--
Lust, Glutton, Pride
And one must hide
Sloth, Wrath and Greed
Even if one is a Swede.
And not to count the dead unless God is on your side.

--

Martin Jackson was an air force captain.
Five years later he became a church chaplain.
Who had a reputation.
For alcohol intoxication.
And a side effect reaction.

--

In the city of Kenora, Ontario, original name Rat Portage, is 124 miles east of Winnipeg.
Originally a territory of the Ojibway who didn't have to beg.
The Stanley Cup was won by the Kenora Thistles in 1907 and included defenceman Art Ross (1886-1964)
A Hockey Hall of Famer and eventually an NHL Boston Bruin boss.
His favourite breakfast meal was bacon, toast and a poached egg.

--

On the Lake of the Woods in Ontario, something went wrong.
With Alberta tourists Patricia and Justin Strong.
When a Conservation Officer noticed that it was dark and their boat had gone.
Were Patricia and Justin still fishing or were they somewhere singing a song?
Before the night was over they were found on one of the islands where they did not belong.
--
Thunder Bay is a city in Northern Ontario adjacent to Lake Superior.
With a population of 122-thousaand and great facilities the city is no longer inferior.
Because of amalgamation of Fort William and Port Arthur the city is happy and cheerier. To work and live it is easier
 Now Thunder Bay is a city like no other with no barrier.
 --
The Saint Lawrence River flows over a rocky bed.
With the New Brunswick just ahead.
When the ship goes Dip. Dip.
And does a flip.
On a most exciting trip I ever had.

The north wind blows along the Canadian east coast.
And I`m the travel adventure host.
Although the traveling adventurers love New Brunswick the most
Until they are surprised to run into a mysterious ugly looking ghost.
Enjoying Starbucks coffee and French toast.
--
When I was in the mountainous Alps.
I met a skier who needed helps.
The snow was so deep.
All he could do is creep.
His name is Jim Phelps.
--
Jacek Malinowski was alone standing on a Poland Krakow City street.
Watching doves and waiting for a friend he was schedule to meet.
When Stella Maslowska came, he held her hand.
Nearby was a 5 piece rock n roll band.
Which played music that was loud but sweet.
--

Krakow is the 2nd largest and one of the oldest cities in Poland.
It`s a leading academic, cultural life in Go-land.
Situated on Wawel Hill, next to the Vistula River, it has grown from a Stone Age settlement to that of an important European city.
Where the residents are witty and pretty.
After you look around, one can take a rowboat and discover Krakow`s Low-land.
--
I decided to take a Caribbean cruise.
When inside the ship I had a snooze.
After I woke up there was lot of booze
And someone had stolen my shoes.
Another cruise I will refuse.
--
On the Columbia River, the rapids roar.
For now and evermore.
With a mighty crash
Our boat makes a splash.
Not like before.
--

The stars are laughing across the sky.
While my wife and I.
On a raft, drift and drift.
And the Rainy River begins to flow swift.
We wonder why and begin to cry.
--
The wind blows from the west.
And destroys a duck`s nest.
So I find a mast.
From the past.
And give the duck a hatching rest.
--
On a Quebec steep hill.
A maple tree couldn't stand still.
While making syrup it sang a lullaby
"Why Oh why must I soon say goodbye?"
And a pail of syrup I don't fill.
--
It's autumn and the tree leaves will fall soon.
And I'll probably see the moon.
As I sweep the leaves that will be a mile high.
Nearly reaching the sky.
Before there's another typhoon.
--

From Edmonton, a city of mine.
Unfortunately I had to decline.
An invitation to travel to Saskatoon.
Where I could see an eclipse of the moon.
Between eight and nine.
--

I know a friend named Conrad Morrow.
Who tomorrow.
Is planning to go fishing on Baker Lake
Instead of having a steak.
'He wants to have a break and enjoy a fish meal without sorrow.
--

In Stewart B. C. there's an apartment structure.
With Aboriginal and Caucasian mixture.
Who each Sunday kneel at an altar.
And pray that their relationship doesn't falter.
And both still love Mother Nature.
--

There are several myths about Canadian rich people.
Who some believe are evil.
Not all wealthy people live in palatial homes.
Made out of brick and stones.
Although many are successful even if they ae not equal.

Rich people are experts in money management.
And some in embezzlement.
They have credit.
Which is difficult to edit.
 If there's a revenue disentanglement.
--
The silver spoon perception of rich people isn't entirely misguided.
They can be decided.
To be divided.
Or one-sided.
If not properly sighted.
--
Starbucks CEO Howard Shultz was raised in a complex for the poor in Brooklyn.
Of course he is good looking.
Talk show host Opera Winfrey was born to a poor family in Mississippi.
And she's not a hippie.
Wealth often depends on being good looking and proper guest booking.
--

Enough of the rich people talk.
It's best I take a walk.
As I'm calm as can be.
 It wasn't until I passed a money tree.
That I find a 100 dollar bill wrapped in a red colored sock.
--
Anyone can go to the Annual Ball.
Including City Council members and that`s not all.
To see the mess.
Reported by journalist Angie Bess.
To see a goofy person crawl a wall.
--
Art
Hart
Is smart
While playing his dart
He knows when not to fart
--
Poet Ed was tired a sore.
Because of his legs he could walk no more.
They ached and pained.
Each day that it rained.
He would fall asleep and snore.
--

Like Rudolph's nose.
My anxiety rose.
Inside and out.
When I was about.
To have an iUniverse book published and was told the high cost, my anxiety rose.

--

Way back when
I saw a birdy wren.
And then a chicken hen
When I saw them again.
I was thankful and to both said, "Amen.``

--

Happy Holidays.
In so many ways.
Christmas is near and soon the days will be longer.
After a heart attack I feel stronger.
And wait for my next pay days.

--

Hello and season`s greetings.
Following several meetings.
Don`t worry and feel sad.
Because Santa is glad.
To help you with Christmas things.

--

Happy New Year to your family train circle.
Even if your family name is Mirckel.
On your train of life your status is beautiful
And in so many ways useful.
Even if you have only one testicle.
--
At the Winnipeg zoo, the tiger was there, the bears too.
They formed a band with a kangaroo.
Along with a couple of beavers and a mouse.
It was like an Open House.
The gophers weren't there because they had the flu.
--
In Winnipeg.
Greg.
Did not want to beg.
So he paid an arm and a leg
To purchase an empty beer keg.
--
Nap who is in charge of our garbage bin.
Emptying what is put in.
He has a big heart.
With his red cart.
 Each Saturday he hauls away the garbage with a grin.
--

At the Burnaby City Hall was an alderman named Gordon Sthal.
Who on a rainy day at a mall purchased a umbrella parasol.
The handle was long.
And even though he was strong.
He couldn't use it at all.
--
Through Facebook.
I met a cook.
Who lived near a brook.
He wasn't a crook.
But once one ate his cooking they had a stomach ache and shook and shook.
--
In the county of Northern Lights lived 16 year old Elsie Korment.
While wearing a bonnet.
Wrote a sonnet.
With rhyming words in it.
When asked for an interview she refused to comment.
--

In the Yukon, a Whitehorse dude.
Says a cool beer tastes good.
If Canadian brewed.
And the food is properly chewed.
Good, No matter what is your mood.
--
Crazy Ville is notorious because of its slums.
Where every weekend a drug pusher comes.
At night time and sometimes even during day time
The peddler makes a sale and commits a crime.
While walking away he sings happy songs.
--
Night time
Is the right time
For a joyful find
And to be kind
And not to commit a crime.
--
Every hour.
I test my willpower.
Not to get angry.
Even it's handy.
As I admire at my favorite flower
--

There were no jokes.
Only a hoax.
On the old folks.
When the caregiver took away their smokes.
And temporally hid them in their night cloaks,
--
Something went wrong
When Josie used a dong
And the same time she sang a song
And her sister came along
And broke the dong which to Josie it did not belong.
--
Victoria was a Victorian.
'First a valedictorian.
After spending time in a sanatorium.
She became a historian.
Specializing in history as Canadian Ukrainian.
--
The other day I felt bad.
'From an experience I had.
When I made my dad.
Terribly sad.
And then mad.
--

Evadne was only.
Lonely.
When she ate a slice of baloney.
And then a pepperoni.
Topped with a spoonful of honey.
--
Take a load off your back.
By removing your packsack.
Instead use a gunny sack
And say: Quack. Quack.
Otherwise you may have a heart attack.
--
Jane went to a store.
Close to the seashore.
Where she purchased a sweater.
And some underwear.
Then she ran out of money and couldn't buy anymore.
--
Always persevere.
Never interfere.
When you hear.
That someone saw me riding a steer.
That is a bit queer.
--

Stanley was a bee keeper
And often a late sleeper.
His problems became deeper
When he became a weeper
And neighbors called him a "Creeper."
--
I think that one or two.
T-shirts is enough for you.
In arranging.
I think of changing.
Something different for you.
--
When I hear the sound of an oncoming train.
Usually it begins to rain.
And I'm unable to train
For our soccer game in Bahrain.
And further develop my soccer brain,
--
I know a girl named Alice,
Who lives in Dallas.
In a condominium named the Palace.
Without malice
She reminds me of a 9th century holy chalice.
--

The Yukon River flows into the Bearing Sea.
On a boat with me was a beautiful lady.
Who I tried to kiss,
But her lips I did miss.
As she said, ``You can kiss anyone else but not me."
--
In the NWT the animals are wild.
Even if the weather is mild.
It's best to be safe, alive.
And to strive.
Even if one is a child.
--
In the Ontario city of Welland, Ed was his way to shop.
And made a sudden stop.
Where he was shaken to the core.
For him a carjacking had not taken place before.
Eventually the jacking attempt was a big flop.
--
In Harrison Hoot Springs, B. C, there was a pest exterminator by the name of Leslie Kerr.
Who exterminated pests with fur.
Also cockroaches, bedbug and ants,
That crawled up one's pants.
Or found in a pile of manure.

Near Moose Lake, Alberta, Lou found a pelican that couldn't fly.
Because of injuries it was about to die.
The bird had a long beak.
And enough food to last a week.
Several days later to the pelican Lou said, Bye, Bye."

--

While boating on Alberta`s Muriel Lake I thought I had made a mistake.
When I heard eerie calls of a loon yodeling and echoing across the lake.
But when I came close to one, I found that the nearly extinct loon is regally patterned in feathers that are black and white.
For me it was a wonderful but not an everlasting sight.
The loon now appears on a Canadian two-dollar coin. A wise decision by the Canadian Mint to make.

--

In the Saskatchewan town of Hudson Bay.
Lives Jay Pompay.
Who each day.
Gets his way.
In harvesting alfalfa, canola and hay.

--

There's an elderly Saskatchewan farmer named McIntyre.
Who is about to retire.
For years he toiled the soil,
Until his blood began to boil.
Eventually he became a liar.

--

Limericks by Edward Lear.
I find a bit queer.
Most of the time he begins the first line with There was.
I suppose it's because.
Mr. Lear was in a constant state of fear.

--

Limerick poet Edward Lear.
Probably couldn't hear.
As most of the time he rhymed line 5
With the same word as on line one that take a dive.
Example: beer rhyming with beer.

--

The limerick is here to stay.
From its curse one can't run away.
One can turn a blind eye.
But no matter how one can try.
It will haunt him/her until their dying day.

--

In Toronto there was a limerick writer named Mandy.
Who wrote limericks about Acer Brandi.
With a pencil or a pen.
She wrote a limerick beginning and ending with Amen.
She wrote that way because Acer was handy.
--
Tyler first experienced a curse.
And then was helped by a nurse.
And did not know which was worse.
The big issue is: to be in a hearse
Or have an empty purse.
--
In the British Columbia village of Kaslo.
On Kootenay Lake, fishing was a bit slow.
So fisherman Tony Zahn.
Read the Koran.
And the fish began to flow.
--

Engulfed by a mountain landscape and dramatic scenery.
In the B. C. village of Kaslo you will not find a coffee beanery.
In the 1800s the community was known for its mining silver and gold.
And now we are told.
Its present attraction is an antique sternwheeler, the Japanese Canadian Museum, nearby Meadow Creek and soon a creamery.

--

In Vancouver's China Town there was a man with a gong.
Who with a mallet kept striking it all day long.
His name is Ding Wong.
However, one day something went wrong,
When he accompanied his gong with an erotic song.

--

Metis Cardinal-Ingle has a problem,
And need help to solve him.
At an Aboriginal function he is laughed at because his skin is not that of an Indian and appears white
At a Canadian function he is laughed at because his skin appears brown and for a true Canadian that isn't right.
Half breed Cardinal-Ingle has a continuous heritage problem.

--

Today is National Coffee Day.
So I enjoy a cup and watch the wind blow the autumn leaves away.
Next month is National Chicken Day.
When I'll sit at table, enjoy breakfast and the eggs chickens lay.
Next is Pay Your Taxes Day, but it will not come until next May.

--

Last week was National Limerick Day.
Celebrating Edward Lear's birthday.
And his 1846 humorous Book of Nonsense.
Which after reading it makes one sing and dance.
To read on the net one doesn't have to pay.

--

Allen Sweet.
Is a storm hunter who lives on 82nd street.
He has chased a hurricane in the state of Maine.
And a tornado in the community of Marwayne.
If lightening is nearby, it is dangerous, and hunter Sweet has to retreat.
--
While in Italy I stopped in Rome.
While under a dome.
I was unlucky in love so I was enjoying a pasta.
When I met curvaceous Shasta.
When I asked for a date, she suggested that I go back home.
--
While in Japan.
I met a radio man.
Who said to me:
"Quick as you can be.
See when the next flight is available to Iran``.
--

When Chester got fired.
He wasn`t inspired.
When hired.
As required.
Because he was too tired.
--
In the B. C. town of Lake Cowichan, there was a man named Rob.
Who had just been fired from his job.
He was angry at his boss.
Who was delighted at the loss.
Because Rob and his friend Bob, belonged to a mob.
--
Here are several great deals.
On the sea or on wheels.
A bus trip to California and the city Santa Cruz.
Or a Caribbean vacation cruise.
In both instances with the special discount, it's an offer one steals.
--

I close my eyes, time can`t erase.
The memory of his loving face.
And all the things that meant so much.
His hearty laugh, his gentle touch.
This part of the legacy he has left me with grace.
--
On our Canadian soil, there is turmoil.
Energy companies are drilling for oil.
This makes come residents boil.
Especially Henry Hoyle.
Who lives on Highway 63 in the Alberta town of Boyle.
--
It's time to vote which is an expression of opinion.
Or a response to a proposed decision.
During an election the verdict is made by casting a ballot and voting
Which at times can be revolting.
Especially when the result isn't to one's liking and the voting tradition is held throughout the entire nation.
--

The new Mayor of Toronto is politician John Howard Tory.
Another Conservative Tory.
Who during an election defeated Doug Ford and Elizabeth Chau.
Who now.
On her election platform of helping the homeless and the poor.
Says, "I'm not sorry."
--
Quality Tower in Halifax is a priciest condo.
Owned by Rene Rondeau.
Who has a pug nose and a bulldog face.
Young ladies does he chase.
Often times it's, pronto.
--
Research engine Google.
Sweeter than a noodle.
You own Google Earth, YouTube, Twitter and more.
So our eyes won`t get sore.
Google. Google. Save the world. If you need help. I play the bugle. My name is Dougal.
--

With an upfront fee.
Your purchase is a guarantee.
Be it milk coffee or tea.
Come and see me.
My name is Jerry.

--

Near Edmonton there were 2 train derailments recently.
Here derailments happen quite frequently.
People protest vehemently.
CN Train Company responds obediently.
And now there is no train wrecks to see.

--

There was a train wreck near the Edmonton community of Astor
That was a historic disaster.
As the train was going faster and faster.
Carrying loads of plaster.
On its way to Jasper.

--

In Edmonton there are over 2000 people who are homeless.
The stat of course is more or less.
Research however, shows many are on social welfare.
To be fair the public seems not to care.
Some even say, "We care less.''

In the Saskatchewan community of Troy.
There was young a boy.
Who wanted to be a cowboy.
Later however, he changed his mind and bought himself a toy.
With the decoy the boy experienced a lot of joy.
--

In the Alberta community of Little Smokey.
Teenager Vernon wanted his career to be hockey.
"Unbelievable!" his father said, ``I think it should be basketball."
"No." Ed replied, "In basketball one has to be tall."
``Then for you in order to win a trophy, try karaoke. ``
--

In Powel River, B. C. Edna hit the right note.
When she put on her coat.
And got off a boat,
 To cast her ballot and vote,
For Alderman Dick Groat.
--

Another Subway fast food restaurant I see.
A restaurant a place for me.
To enjoy Subway food.
That is good.
And almost for free.
--
Peter Dy.
Doesn't want to cry,
The reason why?
He doesn't want to die.
And say, "Goodbye,"
--
In Ottawa, during Question Period, there was an investigation.
Of a government accusation.
The Opposition wanted information about Ghana.
Instead the government gave information about a banana.
Question Period remained in a state of stagnation.
--

When I was eleven.
I dreamt I was in heaven.
And my guardian angel gave me a tour.
Which was exciting that`s for sure.
More exciting than when I had the same tour at age seven.
--
Don't delay!
Order today!
Our special during the month of May.
Is on hairspray.
A 10 percent discount if your name is Faye.
--
In Swan River, Manitoba, there was a security guard, who supposed.
That the garage front door was closed.
But then a large rat.
Ate his hat.
While the security guard dozed.
--
In drinking water from a tap.
One could find himself in a trap.
Because there are various chemicals in the water.
Which could lead one to suffer.
From the chemicals the drink and the other crap.

In Lumby, B. C. there was a squirrel in a pine tree.
Being bothered by a bumble bee.
When a pigeon asked, ``Does the bee buzz?''
The squirrel replied, "It certainly does.
I don't know why it's trying to harm me?"

--

First I was a blusher.
Then a crusher.
Followed by being a lusher.
But the best time was when I became a church usher.
And if during a service parishioners didn't stop talking, I became a door rusher.

--

The entire world is up tight.
Filled with fright.
Money has become tight,
So are tickets for an air flight,
No matter at what height.

--

Numerologists believe the events linked to the time 11:11 can be explained.
The belief is related to the concept of synchronicity and often complained.
Some authors are skeptic and claiming that seeing 11:11 on the clock is an auspicious sign.
Others claim that 11:11 signals a spirit presence when people dine.
And the belief the time 11:11 has a mystical power that is self-contained.
--
Mel is a skateboarding dude.
When he has a spill he becomes rude.
And uses language that is lewd.
At times he even steals food.
That is why Mel is being sued.
--
The Islamic State of ISIS.
In parts of Syria and Iraq is causing a world-wide crisis.
The State is run from oil income to beheadings.
And other terrorist things.
Including setting one on fire, rape and questionable vices.
--

It's true that in Muslim Land.
Writing a limerick is banned.
But with tact.
One can sign a contract.
Just make sure that in it the word Mohammad appears grand.
--
One day when I was a bride I ran to a church inside.
To hide from a stranger that looked like either Jekyll or Hyde
He was carrying a gun.
That's when I decided to run
As nearby there was no security guide.
--
Recently I met a stranger named Holler.
He was 7 feet tall and maybe even taller.
He was handsome and I wished he was smaller.
So his name I did not holler.
To see if he had a Canadian dollar.
--
Suzy was 3 years old.
When she was mauled by a vicious dog.
She needed 10 stiches.
To repair her britches,
At a time it was very, very cold.

I had my hand on my wife's shoulder
And I told her.
That I'm getting older
While she was getting boulder
And I no longer could kiss or hold her
--
There a lot of things the matter with me.
As my health isn't as it should be.
I have arthritis in both knees.
And often I sneeze.
An there are time I have difficulty to see.
--
My pulse is weak and my blood is thin.
I'm sad because of the shame I'm in.
My teeth soon will have to come out.
I cannot hear unless they shout.
And often wonder where have I been.
--
I'm overweight and should become thin.
I worry because of the shape I'm in.
I have arch supports for my feet.
Whenever I walk on a street.
Or dump garbage into the bin.
--

Sleep is denied every night.
And I wake up in a state of fright.
I have demenia and my head begins to spin.
Because of the poor health I'm in.
Even after I take an asprin.
--
The morale of this limerick begins to unfold.
Confirming that I'm getting old.
It's better to say the truth with a grin.
For the poor health that I am in.
Than by someone to be told.
--
Begin.
By marking your pin.
And don't commit a sin.
When you sing.
Begin the Beguine.
--
Forgive the unbelievers that centuries ago
there was a forty day flood.
Which was many years before Robin Hood.
Followed by a seven year famine.
Which even now one should examine himself
if they want to go to heaven.
And not lose any blood.
--

Before I knocked on Masha's private door to enter.
I met Jenny, a beautiful apartment renter.
I felt there was no need for security armour.
As I felt no one would harm her.
As the armour employees were on strike until next December.
--
Joyce.
Had a different voice.
One could have a choice.
To hear her song and rejoice.
Or about Pro Choice.
--
Chichi stood against a wall.
She was beautiful and six feet tall.
And about to fall.
In front of the Community Hall.
When a security guard rescued her and drove to the nearest clinic in a shopping mall.
--
Gloria was near spruce tree.
When she began to behave like a flea.
Between you and me.
She could not see.
A nearby a biting bumble bee.
--

I have searched East and West.
The way that is best.
To build a bird nest.
Without taking a rest.
And not hurting my chest.
--
In Vancouver, there was a man from China.
That was scheduled to meet his long-time friend Nina.
First they fasted.
And then got arrested.
Before moving to Regina.
--
In Toronto there's a man from Mongolia,
Who always carries a magnolia.
It is rude.
Not to eat Mongolian food.
So do so and then say, "Hallelujah!"
--

While at Vancouver's Pacific National Exhibition I attended the Piggy Race.
Three pigs were chasing a rabbit in a competitive chase.
The first piggy half-way, fell down.
The second piggy near the end of the race stumbled and turned around.
The 3rd piggy won the race because before it began it said a prayer with grace.
--
When I'm dead and gone.
My son Sean will come along.
He is healthy and strong.
Employed by Amazon.
And can be relied on.
--
In Pakistan.
When a woman marries a man.
The woman pays fees,
Of a million rupees.
In Newfoundland-Labrador John says.
"I'll be moving there as soon as I can".
--

There's a man in Nairobi.
Who has a strange hobby.
He dresses in a large yellow straw hat.
Sometimes tries to look like an ally cat.
Other times like Mr. Sobey.
--
World News Report --
There's a fatal gun fight in Canada's Parliament Hill.
EBOLA and ISIS dominate World News still.
Edmonton bans total smoking in Churchill Square.
Russia and Venezuela sign as a trading pair.
The West still waiting an Iran promise to fulfill.
--
Russian president Putin continue to thrive on chaos.
Annexed Crimea, military intervention in Ukraine and séance.
With Europe and the Western World finding himself in a bind.
Tourism and oil was a major source of revenue. Now he must find income of a different kind.
Because of his heinous attitude Putin won't be helped by Santa Claus.

Time – Noon.
Soon it will be afternoon
U, S, sending rocket to the moon
With a live racoon
To see if it will eventually croon
--
Time -- Noon plus Minute one
Bun-Bun,
Wants to have fun
So she purchased a water gun
And squirts everyone
--
Time -- One
Time to enjoy a blueberry bun
Kiss my sweet Hun
Before to work I run
Canadian astronaut, Chris Hatfield, says
"Have a good day everyone."
--
Time –- One plus minutes two
By now we had our brew
But we haven't got a clue
How our food to chew
Sorry, Most of us have to go and poo
--

Time -- Two
Between me and you
Time to go to the loo
And on cue
Have a brew with brother Hugh
--
Time – Two plus minutes three
Brandon Lee.
While at sea
Suddenly has to go and pee
 I'm happy it's not me
--
Time - Three
I have a friend who is a Cree
And has a sore knee
So he gave me a key
To get rid of a harassing bumblebee
--
Time -- Three plus minutes four
Jack Fillmore
Was dancing once more
His chore was that his back was sore
And what's more
He was in the hospital once before
--

Time – Four
It was during the Canadian Seven Year War
Jack Franklin Amour
Couldn't ignore his loud snore
Much louder than before
When he belonged to the Diplomatic Corpse
--
Time – Four plus minutes five
Franklin Amour was still alive
After stepping on a noxious beehive
He could dance and do the Jive
While counting to ninety-five
Although in doing so, he had to strive
--
Time -- Five
Burt went for a drive
To have a lake dive
When he ran into a noxious beehive
And was lucky to survive
--
Time – Five plus minutes six
Burt did survive and had a house built out of bricks
And was dating chicks
As an astrologer predicts
Burt will live until age eight-six
--

Time – Six
Catherine Dix
Ran into a bunch of town hicks
Who as usual had their bag of tricks
Catherine wouldn't mix or fix
--
Time –**Six minutes seven plus**
Catherine was employed by Seven-Eleven
Initially she thought she was in heaven
Until she purchased a car that was a lemon
It was a used Ford 2007
--
Time – Seven
Kevin Bevan
When he visited the town of Devon
Thought he was in heaven
Although he was only eleven
--
Time – Seven plus minutes eight
When Kevin grew up he decided to negotiate
With pretty Kate,
A college mate
A quick romantic date
Subject to more than a day or two wold be too late
--

Time – Eight
Young Buddy did not hesitate
To find a date
He could not skate
To create a connection he drove to Westgate
He did find a date, although he was an hour late
--
Time – Eight plus minute nine
One day Nap was feeling fine
And by design
Wrote a limerick 5 line
It was so silly the publishers had to decline
Or be subject to a fine
--
Time – Nine
Susanne Kline
Who is sexy and twenty-nine
Invited me to dine and have a taste of Okanagan wine
Unfortunately the invitation I had to decline
--
Time --Nine plus minutes ten
Susan was a LPN
And taking care of her pet mud hen
Also at the hospital aged men.
One patient was named Barry Ben

Time – Ten
Ken Chen
Was searching for a woman
Resembling a wren
He found one at ESPN
--
Time – Ten plus minute eleven
As soon Ken
Found his woman
The couple went to a den
And now and then,
Both said, "Amen."
--
Time – Eleven
Kevin retires at eleven
And rises up at seven
After dreaming that he had been in heaven
Kevin was wondering what is resin.
--
Time – Midnight
In Yellowknife it's still bright
To play, golf, fish or fly a kite
Midnight is a wonderful sight
To observe the Northern Lights at night
--

Time – Midnight plus minutes twelve
As it was still bright I went to a garage shelve
To check on a car valve
Only to find that it wasn't a bivalve
But a multi-valve
--
Time – One A. M.
Wendy and I went to sleep
My sleep was deep
Wendy however, a promise did not keep
Met a creep
All she did was weep
--
Time – One A. M. plus minutes thirty
When I was thirsty
I found a birdy
That was sturdy
And worthy
But oh so dirty
--

Time – Two A. M.
Lulu
Was in a canoe
With her too
Was Eileen Marcaux
 After an hour Eileen had to say to her,
"Adieu."
--
Time – Two A. M. plus minutes forty
Because of his stature John Short was called,
'Shorty'
Who lived on 2nd Avenue
In Timbuktu
Attending a barbecue
With him too was Betty Lou
Who I knew
--
Time – Three A. M.
We are fiddlers three
Jack, Jill and me
We are performing on a ship while on the sea
To a cubicle I lost our key
Because I could not see
--

Time – Three A. M. plus minutes fifty
Trail, B, C, is known as the Silver City
Where lives sexy Maxie Pixy
Twenty
Pretty and nifty
Can run swiftly but not when tipsy

--

Time Four A. M.
When Geoff was alive
At age twenty-five
He went for a morning drive
To the city archive
On his way his car crashed but Geoff did survive

--

Time – Four A. M. plus minutes fifteen
While driving to the theatre driver Tom was nineteen
Dick, a passenger, was fifteen.
Harry, second passenger, was somewhere in between
The weather was extreme
Although the grass was green

--

Time – Five A. M.
It's five in the morning
The alarm clock gives me a warning
I look out the window without forewarning, it's storming
The rain is pouring
I say to myself "There is no use to be mourning."
--
Time – Five A. M. plus minutes ten
Faith is eight, Hope nine and Charity ten
Parents Mr. And Mrs., Hamm had three children again
Mrs. Hamm was delighted the threesome were girls and not men
So she consulted with fortune teller Glen
Who said, "Congratulations, Looks like you will be broke again"
--
Time – Six A, M.
The house is built of bricks
The number of people living in it is six
Including three chicks
And three hicks
Who on each other play amazing tricks
--

Time – Six A. M. plus minutes eleven
Evelyn lives in the town of Devon
When the clock strikes seven
In a car that is a lemon
She drives to 7-Eleven
Working there is like being in heaven
--
Time – Seven A. M.
In the town of Devon
Is a fast food restaurant owned by Kevin
Which is ready to serve customers at seven
Once you taste his coffee it's like being in heaven

Time -- Seven plus minutes thirty
Clement Purdy
At age 30
Is flirty
His hands are always dirty
To know him better isn't worthy
--
Time Eight A. M.
It's eight
I enjoy breakfast and open the gate
In search for a possible date
By noon I found charming Kate
But I was a bit late

Time – Eight A. M. pus minutes thirteen
A passenger during a car drive, Velma was thirteen
Linda nineteen
Thelma somewhere in between
Velma and Linda were always clean
While Thelma at times was angry and mean
--
Time – Nine A. M.
At High School the closest friend of mine
Was Elizabeth Klein
Some days at nine
Together we would enjoy a glass of wine
Both would always toe the line

Time -- Nine plus minutes twenty
Monty
At twenty
On street 120
In a land of plenty
Lives next to Milton Huntley.
--

Time – Ten A. M.
Eight, nine, ten
Let the limerick contest begin
We need at least ten
Contestant again
With a pencil or a pen
--
Time – Ten plus minutes thirty-two
Between me and you
I'm a Jew
Which I thought you knew
This town has only few
Our anti-Semitism needs a review
--
Time – Eleven A. M.
Nine, ten, eleven
Let's get in the spaceship destined for heaven
We'll pass many stars
And planet Mars
And reach our destination on day seven
--
Time – Eleven plus minutes thirty-six
In hockey Quincy wears number 96
At age 26
He's full of tricks
Opposing players he licks
With his hockey sticks

Mr. and Mrs. Bundy
In their Hyundai
Drive to church each **Sunday**
On Monday its Relax Day
So they drive into the country to enjoy an ice-cream sundae

--
Mr. and Mrs., Lundy.
With their neighbours Mr. And Mrs. Gundy
Drove to Bay of Fundy.
And fished for most part of **Monday**.
And didn't return home until the following Thursday

--
Mary Gundy.
A beauty.
On **Tuesday**,
Because of difficult circumstances had to delay.
Celebrating her 21st birthday.

--

Sunday is Church Day
Monday is School Day
Tuesday is Remembrance Day
Wednesday is Pay Day
Thursday is Spending Day
--
Ray in Hudson Bay
Faye in Bombay
Two love birds did not meet on **Thursday**
Because of a lengthy flight delay
To meet soon, each knelt and pray
 --
It was on a July **Friday**
On her birthday
Coleen Day
Thought, "Since I'm driving on a unknown highway
I'll drive my way"
--
Its **Saturday** hockey night
We attend the Battle of Alberta game and see a fight
As soon as the game is over we have a party
Where my husband and I will discuss my salary
My penicillin allergy and of course, the fight
--

(A) Jack and Sprat live in Hudson Bay
During the month of May
Jack works at eBay
While Sprat is suffering from a tooth decay
In the morning both pray
--
(B) Ravi
A war amputee
Always votes NDP
After having gone to pee
He enjoys a cup of Tim Horton's coffee
--
(C) Allan McPhee
Is a MC
With a degree
In Economy
And a friend of Wayne Gretzky
--
(D) Joseph Cardinal is a Native Cree
At age 33
A security employee
That has the Master Key
To the house tree
--

(E) Deedee Kennedy
Is an employee
At the Public Library
Minutes ago she helped members find
information about Trans Canada Energy
For free
--
(F) Jeff
Initially was a hockey ref
Then became a restaurant chef
Supervising a ten-member staff
Seldom do they make a gaffe
--
(G) Dee, Bea and Mari
A group of three
Living in B. C.
Each with a Masters' degree
Are exploring the Arctic Beaufort Sea
--
(H) Henry Cage
Became of age
And then at a theatre back stage
Worked for a minimum wage
At that time was the rage
--

(I) Lisa a foreign contract worker in Dubai
Her employer abused her and made her cry
She found a gun
When her work was done
She said to her co-workers "Bye, Bye Dubai."
--
(J) Jay
A Toronto Blue Jay
In May
With Jose was involved in a fray
Minutes later everything was okay.
--
(K) Today
Fifteen year old Kay
Was helping her father with the hay
It was mid-day that she didn't want to stay
An hour later she ran away
--
 (L) Edith Bell
Met garbage collector Eric Snell
Edith, a saleslady, complained about Eric's objectionable smell
And was reluctant to go out and sell
Eric's response was, "Edith, sorry I don't feel well."
--

(M) It was about eleven P. M.
When Oliver turned on radio CJAM FM
For the latest Edmonton Oilers/Calgary hockey scores played that Sunday
And Monday
When the score was announced Oliver exclaimed, "Whoopee. Oilers beat them!"
--
(N) Japan
Is a member of ASEAN
Sending workers where it can
At the oil sands project near Fort McMurray there are ten
Five drivers and five brakemen
Including Ben and Ken
--
(O) A short while ago
Business at the Come and Go cafeteria was slow
Because of the large amount of snow
Streets were plugged and nowhere to go
Manager Bo wanted to go out but the waitresses pleaded, "No, no!"
--

(P) Didn`t you see?
The Halloween tricks they played on me?
My huge pumpkin they hung on a tree
For everyone to see
Except my wife and me
--
(Q) A short time ago
A UFO
Was heading towards Toronto
The other to Chicago
Where else, I don't know
--
(R Shirley McFar, a Hollywood star
Purchased a used car
While enjoying a chocolate bar
She paid for the lemon car
But it did not go far
--
(S) Mr. and Mrs. Hess
Live in the U. S.
I must confess
Mrs. Hess is in distress.
Each time she wears a yellow dress
--

(T) Between you and me
Jason Cowrie
Lives in B, C.
Near the sea
Where by a tree he enjoys listening to his musical CD
--
(U) I wish I knew
Why each Saturday night I feel blue
And it's true
Between me and you
I don't know what to do
--
(V) A robin near me
Sat on a spruce tree
So happy was he
Singing "Hi dee- dee"
For free.
--
(W) Custodian supervisor Hermes Yu
Has cleaning staffs of 22
At Lilly Osborne High School
He's a jewel
Cleaning done, to each cleaner he says, "Thank you."
--

(X) Brothers Hecht's.
Are architects.
On 2 different projects.
And sign their cheques with an X.
They can speak 6 different dialects.
--
(Y) Cy
In July
Was near the sky
When he got poked in the eye
And began to cry
--
(Z) Fred
To Ed
Said: "Your face is getting red.
Buy a loaf of bread
Enjoy a sandwich and then go to bed."

(A-Name) The first man on Planet Earth was Adam.
In Toronto there's a man named McAdam.
Who at random.
Was handed a memorandum.
To go and help the poor in Siam.
--

(B-Name) Jerry Barry.
Lived in Glengarry.
While having breakfast he enjoyed a strawberry.
His problem however, was dietary.
A medical consultation was necessary.
--
(C-Name) Chelsie Mackenzie.
Wasn't healthy
After visiting Haiti she called on her sister Elise.
Who was wealthy.
Together they enjoyed Boston Pizza spaghetti.
--
(D-Name) Dick was dressed like a suburban hick.
He was obviously sick.
The things he participated in never seemed to click.
Even his most reliable trick
Using a two-foot magic stick.
--

(E-Name) God gave Adam, wife Eve.
And not Steve.
Together they had two sons Abel and Caine.
In the main.
Cain killed his brother causing God lot of grief.
--
(F-Name) Frank.
Was a Yank who continually whiskey drank.
And wasn't frank
When he went to see his savings bank.
After seeing his account his heart sank.
--
(G-Name) In Alabama there's a town called Tuskegee.
With a 125 year-old university.
Recently granting a post graduate degree.
To 25-year-old Guy Gee.
In his final exam, for an example, he marked the page with an e. g.
--

(H-Name) A young friend of mine named Aldrich.
Worked in Bangladesh.
When he became of age.
Worked in a clothing factory for less than the minimum wage.
Eventually Aldrich fell into a fit of rage.
--
(I-Name) In Toronto there's a married couple named Mie and Pie.
As Filipino immigrants they were shy.
It was during the month of July.
That Mie felt homesick and began to cry.
Pie wondered: "My Oh my. I wonder why?"
--
(J-Name) Andrea is wealthy and enjoyed traveling world-wide. First to Estonia.
Then Bulgaria, China and Ethiopia.
India, Libya, Latvia.
Saint Lucia, Sri Lanka and Syria.
Andrea's final trip at 80 was to Mesopotamia.
--
(K-Name) Today, Kay.
Decided to pray.
Because she did disobey.
A Los Angeles hotel valet.
A friend of Danny Kay.

(L-Name) Mademoiselle Elle.
Is a decedent of Alexander Graham Bell.
One could not tell.
She owns an Alberta oil well.
And enjoys listening to the music of Swiss, William Tell.
--
(M-Name) Emma lives on the Isle of Man.
And said, "As soon as I can.
I must marry a handsome man."
Eventually she found Dan.
And together to the pastor they ran.
--
(N-Name) Hanna from Montana.
Lived in Louisiana.
And had a passion for a banana.
Even after she moved to Indiana.
And then to Alabama.
--
O-Name) A Russian lady named Olga.
Swam in the River Volga.
Aside from swimming she enjoyed dancing the polka.
After enjoying a cola. She met Viola.
Both then met with an Ayatollah and tried to curb EBOLA
--

(P-Name) Mr. and Mrs. Gee.
Were sitting by a palm tree.
Facing the Mediterranean Sea.
Between you and me.
As it was foggy it was difficult for them to see.
--
(Q-Name) Hugh.
At thirty-two.
Had a high IQ.
While doing a literary review.
Always said, "For you. Thank You."
--
(R-Name) When Tommy Farr.
Lived in Qatar.
He was a super star.
Playing the kazoo and the guitar.
He was the best by far.
--
(S-Name) Less and Bess.
Lived in Buffalo, U. S.
Where they met Don Pless
And Arthur Hess
Whose life was in an awful distress
--

(T-Name) 60-year-old Timothy.
Lived in the Alberta town of Thorsby.
And said: "There must be.
A better place to retire," so he went to Haiti.
But he couldn't speak French and there was a terrible earthquake so he retired in the Pacific paradise of Tahiti.

--

(U-Name) In the Alberta town of Picture Bute.
On his home route with little loot.
Henry saw a coyote.
And was ready to shoot.
For the wild coyote it was kaput.

--

(V-Name) My friend Steve.
Married Eve.
Then it was hard to believe.
Steve had a terminal leave.
This led Eve to grieve.

--

(W-Name) Benjamin is a Jew.
In Bonnyville there are only two.
Ben owns a convenience store.
Abe a clothing store.
For Joe they are the most honest merchants he ever knew.

(X-Name) Ruth's ex.
Signed his cheques.
With an X.
After their marriage went wrong due to a hex.
About sex.

--

(Y-Name) In India's city of New Delhi.
Ever since he was knee high.
Cy wanted to become an espionage spy.
As an adult he went to Dubai.
Where he was caught and began to cry.

--

(Z-Name) No matter how you pronounced the letter Z, In America is as Zee and in Canada as Zed.
In Canada 11-year-old Alfred.
To his mother said:
"Please bring me a slice of cinnamon bread.
And then I'll go to bed."

In the morning, about ten o'clock.
There's a knock.
On the 2nd door.
Of the main floor.
It's a neighbor alerting there was a house fire on the next block.

Grace.
Dressed in lace.
Had a sad face.
As she came 2nd place.
In the one-mile race.

--

Dolly Dimple.
Has a pimple.
And walks like this,
For a kiss.
That is simply simple.

--

I said, "Hello sir.
To Phil. Our grocer.
What is your price
For a sack of rice?"
His response was: "Sorry. The rice was destroyed by a pack of mice."

--

Jumping Joan.
At her home.
While alone.
Began to moan.
Because someone had hit her head with a stone.

--

I asked my parents for fifty cents.
To see an elephant jump a fence.
It was during July.
That the elephant nearly reached the sky.
To me that was a small expense.

--

The most powerful person in ancient Egypt was the Pharaoh.
He was the political and religious leader whose power wasn't narrow.
His title was Lord of the Two Lands.
And he collected taxes with his own hands.
And defended Egypt against foreign invasion like there was no tomorrow.

The **Bible – (Genesis 1 – 94)** --
In the beginning God created heaven and the earth which was without form and empty. And not plenty.
Darkness was everywhere so God said: "Let there be light and there was light and He Separated the light from darkness. God called the light, day and darkness night.
And there were day and evening on the 1st day.
And He did not stop to make the earth his way.
On the 2nd day God said, "Let there be a sky in the midst of the waters," And divided the waters candidly.
--
On the 3rd day God said, "Let the waters under heaven be gathered together in one place and let dry land appear.`` God called the dry land Earth and the waters he called it Sea. This began with the Mediterranean Sea.
 And then God said, "Let the Earth bring forth grass, and yield plants bearing seed, and the trees fruit.``
On the 4th day God said: "Let there be lights in the sky of heaven to divide the day from

the night and let there be four seasons –
spring, summer, autumn and winter."
If by then there were people on the earth, they
would give a hoot.
For the likes of you and me.

--

On the 5th day God said: "Let the waters
bring forth in great numbers moving creatures
that have life, and birds that fly the earth.``
So God created whales and birds and every
living creature that moves. Hr blessed them
And said, "Be fruitful and multiply, and fill
the waters of the seas, Let the birds also
multiply on earth."
And blessed them that they give multiple
birth.

--

On the 6th day God said: "Let the earth bring
forth creatures of all kinds, cattle, creeping
things and beasts, and make man in my
image, with the power.
Over everything that moves on earth. And
doesn't go sour.``
So God created man and woman, male and
female, in his own image and blessed them by
saying, "Be fruitful, multiply and have power.

Over every living thing that moves on earth
and I'll be watching every hour.
"Yes, every hour."
On the 7th day the making of heaven and
earth was completed so God took a rest.
 And made it a holy day for everyone to rest.
God had made man from the dust of the
ground and breathed into him the breath of
life and thus man became a living soul.
Which he was to control.
Even if one lived in the West.

--

After creation, in the Garden of Eden.
 A long distance from present Sweden.
A woman disobeyed God and ate the
forbidden apple.
This caused God to rattle.
Because a serpent advised the woman to eat
the apple for the wrong reason.

--

To the woman God said: "For eating the
forbidden fruit, I will multiply your suffering,
And make you an offering.
Your husband shall rule over you.
And your children too.
Which you may find puzzling.``

--

Adam, the first man on Planet Earth, named his wife Eve.
And not like some believe it was Steve.
They had 2 sons Cain and Abel
Cain eventually killed his brother Abel.
That caused God a lot of grief.

--

Cain eventually was forgiven and while in the land of Nod,
This may seem odd.
Eve gave birth to another son Seth, to replace Abel.
And make Eve's life more stable.
For herself and all her descendants including Maude.

--

Adam lived to a very old age on Planet Earth.
At the time no one knew what it was worth,
By now there were many descendants.
Given independence.
One was Noah who had three sons: Shem, Japbeth and Ham by birth.

--

Man had become wicked and evil so God said to Noah, "Make a 3 deck arch
 Out of wood. For there shall be a flood."
The flood wasn't to do any good.

Entering the arch all were in pairs: birds, beasts and creeping things.
Like the killer bee that stings.
Although there was a mighty rain storm, there was no loss of blood.

--

Rain fell 40 days and nights until Noah's arch rested on the peak of Mount Ararat.
That's when Noah said, "Now what?"
God blessed Noah and his sons and said to them, "Be fruitful. Multiply and replenish the earth.``
After 40 days the flood had receded and the earth now had a new worth.
Multiply everything that lives, including fish in the sea aftermath.

--

After the flood Noah was an old man when he died.
His sons and their sons cried.
However, God had already vowed.
That the sons and their dependents would be fathers of the earth and placed a rainbow to be seen in the cloud.
To prove God had made a promise and had not lied.

After God made an agreement with Noah, his decedents increased greatly.
And at that time they had only one language which was stately.
And they said, "Let's build a city with a tower whose top may reach heaven, and call it Babel,"
There was confusion as there was only one language so God decided to scatter the dependents over the face of the earth, including what now is known as Italy.
--

In the Land of Haran lived descendent Abraham to whom God made a promise
This would not be ominous.
For Abraham to leave Haran and he and his family and their decedents, would not be harassed.
But joyfully blessed
And live in a state of bliss.
--

Abraham at age 75 agreed to God's promise and with his wife Sarah and his brother's son Lot, went to live in the land of Canaan.
But at the time in Canaan there was a famine.
So Abraham spent 5 years in Egypt and came back when the famine was over.
And there was plenty of clover.
God's wish Abraham did not abandon.
--
Abraham had a vison.
And it wasn't on television.
And God gave Abraham land to inherit.
Without merit.
And as the sun was going down, a deep sleep and darkness fell on him.
To Abraham God said, "In the land I gave, your children shall be in bondage and oppressed for 400 years.
And the nation that oppresses them, I'll be the judge. And your children with emerge with a great possession and those who oppress them shall be in tears.
You yourself shall go away in peace and buried at an old age while your children shall return in the 4th generation.
And remain as the same nation.
Without any fears.``

When Abraham was 90 years old, God said to him, "Walk in my ways, be perfect and I'll give you an everlasting covenant that your people will increase greatly.
And it will be done stately.
And you and you children I'll give you land in Canaan,
As part of my covenant, your wife Sarah will have a child and every male descendant shall be circumcised when 8 days old.``
And upon God's covenant, Abraham was sold.
And appreciated by descendant Shannon Buchanan.

Abraham obeyed the Lord's command and was given a test directing him to offer his son Isaac, as a holocaust.
At no cost.
When Abraham was about to kill Isaac an angel appeared from heaven and pleaded:
Abraham! Abraham! Do not lay a hand on the boy.
Because Isaac is your son to enjoy.
God you must trust.``
--

Since Abraham didn't kill his son, God asked him to find Isaac a wife.
To be with him all his life.
It was at a spring well that Rebecca appeared with a water pitcher on her shoulder.
Seeing beautiful Rebeca, Isaac became boulder.
And took a golden ring of half shekel weight, and 2 bracelets also of gold, and took Rebecca to his mother's tent. A short time later they became husband and wife.

--

After a long life Abraham died and buried in the cemetery cave of Macphela next to Sarah his wife.
Their dependants cried.
When Isaac was 30 Rebecca bore him 2 sons – Esau and Jacob.
Esau was hairy and strong while Jacob was skinny, mild and weak.
As adults Esau hated Jacob and plotted against him because his father blessed him because he was meek.
Esau forced Jacob to sell his birthright to him, and soon as he did, Jacob fled to the land before he died and Abraham gave him, but still he had to struggle with his life

After Jacob had fled he had a dream that there was a ladder reaching heaven and angels were on it.
And the Lord was standing above the ladder and had said to him: "The land which you lie I will give to you and your children and they shall be the dust of the earth
Not in mirth.``
When Jacob woke from his sleep it was past seven.
And said: "Surely this is the house of God and this is the gate to heaven.
The stone I used as a pillow will be in God's house, and all that you give to me, O God, I will give you a tenth to you to make certain that you stay fit.``
Jacob went on his journey and came to the land of the people of the East
where near a well were 3 herds of sheep.
Although short of sleep.
Jacob asked the shepherds, "My brothers where are you from?"
They said, "We are from Haran."
From then on Jacob had a lot of information to keep.
--

One of the questions asked the shepherds was.
"Do you know Laban, the son of Nahor?
They said, "We know him and more.``
Then Jacob asked, "Is all well with him?"
And they answered, "All is well and look,
there's his daughter Rachel, herding her
father's sheep."
As soon as Jacob saw beautiful Rachel he
kissed her and began to weep.
And then told Rachel that he was her father's
kin and that his knees from continuous
praying began to get sore.

--

Laban hastened to meet Jacob, his sisters son,
embraced, kissed and brought him inside his
father's house.
Unknown to Laban, Jacob was in search of a
spouse.
Laban had 2 daughters, Leah and Rachel.
After working for 7 years for Laban he said
that Jacob could have Rachel and he was
grateful.
Because also after Rachel's affection was
suitor Clause.

--

At the end of seven years Jacob said to Laban, "Please give me Rachel because I have fulfilled our agreement."
Jacob thought there could be abandonment. Meanwhile Laban prepared a wedding feast but that evening because of darkness, he instead brought Leah to Jacob and married her believing she was Rachel.
When Jacob discovered that he had been tricked he said to Laban, "What have you done to me? Did I not deserve to have Rachel?
I need your acknowledgement.``

--

Laban said to Jacob, "If you promise to work for another 7 years I'll give you Rachel too.
Jacob however, loved Rachel more than he loved Leah. Rachel did not bear any children And he was unhappy while Leah gave him a son.
The Lord took pity on Rachel and allowed her to bear one and she named him Joseph, the only one.
After 20 years with Laban, Jacob prospered exceedingly well like he never knew.

--

Jacob and Laban made a pact before he parted.
And were quick to act as the agreement started.
Then Jacob said to the men with him, "Gather stones and make a heap."
They did little sleep.``
And partied all night with Laban kissing his grandsons and daughters.
Early in the morning Laban rose, blessed everyone and returned to his land from which he started.

--

While Jacob was on his way to Canaan an angel of God met him and sent a message to Esau, his brother.
Who was a bit older.
Esau acknowledged the message that he will meet Jacob accompanied with his 400 men.
Divided in camp # 1 and # 2 camp.
For brother Esau in an agreement had promised to give Jacob's berth rite back along with 220 goats, and 220 sheep, 30 milking camels and 10 bulls, 40 cows, 30 asses to which Esau had approved with a stamp.

When Jacob was left alone he met an angel who said to him, "Your name will no longer be Jacob but **Israel** and no other.``
--
When Esau arrived he said, "Jacob, what do you mean by giving m all this flock?"
"They are to find grace in the sight of my Lord.`` Jacob said.
Esau shook his head but finally agreed, accepted the gift and said: "Let us continue our journey and I will go to Seir and you to Canaan." Before they departed Esau said to Jacob, "I will you some of my men as you may find the journey rough.``
After living in Canaan for some time, Rachel bore Jacob son that was named Benjamin.
A short time later Rachel died and was buried near Bethlehem, Jacob, an experienced hunter, took care of Benjamin and his cattle stock.
--
Joseph, a stranger, dealt in the land that his father had been in Canaan.
Now considered to be Lebanon, Israel, Palestine and parts of Syria and Jordan.
Joseph, strong and healthy, daily fed the stock with his brothers and one day brought an evil

report to his father, that he loved him more than his other sons, so his father made him a coat of multicolor.

When the other brothers realized their father loved Joseph more than them, they hated Joseph and their relationship became duller. It became even worse when Joseph dreamed a dream and told it to his brothers that the sun, the moon and stars bowed to him. They hated him all the more and threatened to kill him in Canaan.

--

Joseph's brothers were envious and threw him into an empty water pit.

And sat down to eat bread and behold, they saw a caravan of Ishmaelite's (decedents of Ishmael, the elder son of Abraham) loaded with spices, balm and myrrh, on its way to Egypt, and they could not sit.

Then Judah said to his brothers, "Let us not touch Joseph for he is our flesh and in good fit.``

That satisfied the brothers, they took his coat, killed a goat and dipped the coat of many colors in blood and sold Joseph to the Ishmaelite merchants for 20 pieces of silver.

For this unusual action the brothers did not shiver.
When father Jacob found out what had happened he refused to be comforted and with tears said, "I will grieve for my son and never quit."
--
Joseph was brought into Egypt where Potiphar, a captain and a guard, bought him from the Ishmaelite's. The Lord was with Joseph and he became a favourite servant living in the house of the Egyptian Master, In the end the experience was a disaster, Joseph a handsome young lad, when he grew up, his Master's wife loved him, but Joseph didn't love her and said. "Behold the Master doesn't even know what is in the house because you are his wife. How could I love you and do this wickedness and sin against God?"
And then there was a fraud.
As the wife went to the Master and lied by telling him that Joseph wanted to harm her. When the Master heard what his wife had said, he put Joseph into a prison.

But God showed mercy and the keeper put all the prisoners in charge of Joseph which Included several spies.
With eyes of a large size.
--
It happened later that the butler and his baker offended their Pharaoh, the king of Egypt. In his anger he put both into prison and Joseph stood guard over them,
It was approximately 10:00 P. M.
One night the butler and baker each had a different dream, but could not find anyone Interpret them so Joseph said, "Well, tell me you dreams."
The butler said: 'A vine was before me and on the vine 3 branches. It seems.
They budded and the blossoms shot forth into clusters in a basket that was on my head.
Joseph to the butler then said, "The 3 branches are 3 days. Within 3 days the Pharaoh will restore you into your original position with haste.`` And continued: "I beg of you to mention to the Pharaoh to get me out of this place as I deserved not to be in this dungeon as it's an called for scam.``
--

When the chief baker saw the butler's interpretation, he said to Joseph, "I also had a dream and behold I had 3 baskets on my head.``

And Joseph said:

The interpretation of your dream that the 3 baskets are 3 days, Within 3 days the Pharaoh will call and hang you on a tree and the birds will eat of your flesh.``

On the 3rd day which was Joseph's birthday and the interpretations were still fresh. Pharaoh made a feast for all his servants. He called for the butler and gave the baker a cup but he hanged the baker and it was as Joseph had said.

The Pharaoh had a dream and stood by the river and behold 7 fat cows came out of the Nile.

But the Pharaoh did not smile.

Then behold 7 scrawny cows got rid of the fat cows and when Pharaoh slept again and had a 2nd dream 7 scrawny ears under size, sprang after them, and the 7 undersized ears devoured the 7 hard and full ears.

When Pharaoh woke up he realized it was only a dream and wasn't in shock.

But his spirit was disturbed so the following morning he called all wise men and magicians in Egypt, but there no one who could interpret the dreams so he sent for Joseph and he came out of the dungeon and to the Pharaoh said: "It's not in my power but God shall give you the answer in a short while."

--

Next day Joseph said to Pharaoh, "Your both dreams have the same meaning by God. The 7 cows and the 7 corn ears are years of plenty. The 7 thin cows and 7 empty corn ears will be 7 years of famine." Which to Pharaoh seemed odd.
"What God is about to do is show you there will be 7 years of greatness throughout Egypt and after them will come 7 years of famine and God will make this happen soon."
Meanwhile the same afternoon:
The Pharaoh searched for a man that is wise and discreet and appointed Joseph governor of Egypt and let his me gather food and store it in cities to use at the time of the famine.
The plan sounded reasonable for the Pharaoh and most of his servents. Although several were awed.

--

Several days later Pharaoh said to Joseph: "In as much God has showed you all this.
There is no one as wise and discreet as you are. You shall be in charge of my house and all the people will be ruled according to your word this day on.
Only on the house itself will I be greater than you. I have just named you all over the land of Egypt beginning at the next dawn.``
Pharaoh took off his ring from his hand at put it on Joseph's, and the dressed him in robes of fine linin and put a gold chain around his neck.
Then he made Joseph ride in the second royal chariot and said, "I'm Pharaoh and no man will lift his hand or foot in all of Egypt and make you a wreck."
Then Pharaoh gave Joseph the Egyptian name of Zaphnath-Pamea and for his wife Asnath, the daughter of Potipherah, the priest of Zon.
--
Joseph was 30 years old when he toured all of Egypt. In the years of plenty there was food in abundance and Joseph gathered it, and stored it in cities and locations nearby.
He grain quantities that he had lost count and no one did cry.

Meanwhile wife Asenath gave Joseph 2 sons before the year of the famine and they were named Manasseh and Ephraim.

The 7 years of plenty ended and the 7 years of poverty began. In Egypt there was bread for the people of Egypt while rest of earth famished but not because of him.

Because that is when Joseph opened the store houses and people from all countries came to Egypt to buy food from him so that no one would die.

--

Jacob had heard that there was grain in Egypt and said to his sons: "Go buy some food for us so that we may live and not die.``

So Joseph's 10 brothers set out to buy grain in Egypt but Joseph's younger brother Benjamin, did not go for fear of being harmed and that he may die.

When they arrived to buy grain Joseph accused his brothers of being spies.

The brothers denied the allegation and were put into prison for 3 days and where Joseph said, "Do this and save your lives.

One of you stays in prison and the rest take the grain to feed the hungry in your houses, but bring your missing brother to me that your words are proven and no one shall cry.``

--

When the brothers reached home they emptied their bundles and found their money inside and became afraid.
So Jacob said, "Look. You have taken away my children – Joseph and Simon are no more, and now you want Benjamin to the Egyptian store. All these things are against me." So he prayed.
That's when Rueben said to his father, "You can kill my 2 sons if I do not bring Benjamin back to you. Put him into my hand and I will bring him back again".
But Jacob was with some pain.
And said,
"No. My son shall not go with you for his brother is already dead and he alone is left. If harm should come to him you would bring down my sorrow to the grave.``

--

The famine continued and time came when Jacob and his sons had eaten the grain which they had bought in Egypt and then their father said to them: "Go and buy us some food. But son Judah said to him, "If you will send brother Benjamin with us, we will go and buy food. On the other hand if you don't, the man had said, 'You shall not see my face unless your brother is with you.''

Judah then asked his father, "Isn't that good?" And continued, "Please send Benjamin with me and we shall go so that we may not die". In return Jacob said to him, "If it must be, do this: take some fruit of the land and carry them to the man, presents of balm, honey myrrh, nuts and almonds, and give the money back because it may have been an oversight and you should deny.'' A short time later they took the presents, money and Benjamin and stood before Joseph, requesting food that should be good.

--

Joseph saw Benjamin and said to the ruler of the house: "Take these men to my house and we will dine at noon.'' The servant took the brothers to Joseph's house during a full moon. Inside the brothers were afraid and one said, "Is it because of the money we returned in our sacks that we have been brought here, so the he may find fault with us and make us slaves? We do not know who put the money in our sacks.'' The servant said, "Fear not, your

God, the God of your father gave you the treasure in your sacks.``
And brought Simon to them and gave water to wash their feet.
Meanwhile they prepared to give presents to Joseph. They bowed before him and he asked them. "Is your father still alive?"
Joseph spotted Benjamin and asked the men. Is this your younger brother whom you told me?"
When the said it was, Joseph went to his room and wept. Minutes later he returned and to the servant and said, "Serve the food as it is now noon.``
--

The servants served Joseph separately and the brothers by themselves, and the Egyptians who ate also, by themselves, because Egyptians could not eat bread with Hebrews for that Was against Egyptian law.
And included any Hebrew in-law.
The brothers sat in front of Joseph and looked at each other in wonderment when Benjamin was served 5 times as much as any of the others. They drank and were merry and then Joseph gave an order to the steward by

saying, "Fill the men sacks with food and put their money back into their sacks without a flaw.``
In the morning they were sent away and Joseph said to the steward, "Follow the men and when you overtake them say, "Why have you returned evil for good? It's an unwritten law.
Is this not the cup from which my lord drinks? In doing this you have done evil which no one saw."

--

The steward overtook the brothers and spoke the words of Joseph, but they asked him:
"Why does the lord say these things?
What good to him it brings?"
Behold the money we found in our sacks we brought back to the lord from the land of Canaan. Why then would we steal silver and gold of the lord's house?
Maybe it was someone's spouse?"
Let who ever among us be found guilty and die, and the rest of us become the lord's slaves.
This is the most ridiculous comment that leaves us with stings.``

--

The steward to the men did say, "Though it might be true what you say. He who has the cup shall be the lord's slave but rest of you will be blameless.
And not have any stress.``
Then each brother opened his sack, the steward searched, and the cup was found in Benjamin's sack.
And now there was no turning back.
A then Joseph said, "The man who has the cup shall be my slave. As for the rest of you, go in peace to your father as you had left my house in a mess.``
--
Joseph to everyone said, "Now please leave me.``
So the Egyptians departed and Joseph made himself known to his brothers.
Amid some disorders.
He said, "Brothers, come close to me and I will tell you that I'm Joseph, your brother, who sold me to Egypt. Now do not grieve or get angry because you sold me because God sent me here to preserve your families on earth. It wasn't you who sent me here but God.
And he did not use a whipping rod.

But made me an advisor to the Pharaoh over the Egyptian land. sea and those in poverty."
--
News of the event pleased Pharaoh and his servants. Pharaoh said to Joseph: "Say to your brothers: 'Load your beasts and hurry to Canaan. Get your father and come to see me and I will give you the best land in Egypt and you shall eat of the fat of the land."
The brothers said, "Yes, we understand.``
The brothers came to Canaan to see Jacob their father, all that Joseph had said.
Jacob's heart grew.
Faint for he could not believe what Joseph had said but they told him every word was true.
Jacob then said: "Fine our journey will be accompanied by a band.
--
Jacob left for Beersheba with everything he owned and offered sacrifices to God of his father Isaac.
Who at one time had a large sack.
God spoke to Jacob at night during a dream and said, "I'm the God of your father. Do not fear by going to Egypt for I will establish you there as a great nation, I will go with you to

Egypt and pick you up after Joseph has closed his eyes.``

Jacob departed from Beersheba and his sons carried him, their little ones and their wives in wagons which Pharaoh had sent to carry them. And along the way there were a number of highs.

Jacob came to Egypt and all his kindred with him, his sons, daughters and sons of sons, his daughters and their sons' daughters and on the way there were no surprising attack.

--

Jacob came to Goshen and Joseph made ready his chariot. After Joseph introduced himself he wept, so his father said: "Now I may die since I have seen your face and know you are alive".

Joseph took 5 of his brothers and presented them to Pharaoh who asked, "What is your occupation in order to survive?"

And they answered: "We are shepherds and pray that on account of the famine in Canaan to let us live in Goshen."

Pharaoh turned to Joseph and said to him, "Your father and your brothers have come to live in Goshen. If you know of any great me of great value among them, make them

overseers of cattle that belong to me. If you can I would like to speak to them before ten.``
Joseph brought his father and introduced him to Pharaoh at five.

--

Joseph placed his father and brothers in the land of Rameses part of Goshen as Pharaoh had ordered. Now that the famine was everywhere both in Egypt and Canaan people were
Sad.
There was no money left so the Egyptians came to Joseph and said, "Please give us food before we get mad."
Joseph said, "Give me your cattle in exchange and I'll give you bread.`` So they made an exchange and since there was no improving in sight Joseph bought their land and removed the land title and only the priests kept theirs instead.
Joseph made it a law that from now on Pharaoh will have the fifth part from every harvest except from the priests so that they would be happy when they went to bed they would have a dream, best they ever had.

--

Jacob who was called Israel, lived in Egypt for 17 years until he was about to die and to son Joseph said, "Do not bury me in Egypt but where Abraham and his wife Sarah and where they buried Isaac and Rebekah and I buries Leah.
Which is near the Mediterranean Sea.
He then called his 12 sons: Reuben, Simon, Levi, Judah, Issacharm, Zebulun, Benjamin, Dan, Napthali, Gad and Joseph and blessed each one.
This done.
Joseph said, "Your wishes I shall agree.``
When Jacob died he was buried in the Machpela cave and the Egyptians mourned for 40 days.
And from then on Jacob was an earth absentee.
Now that Jacob was dead.
Joseph to his brothers said:
"Fear not that I'm here in place of God. You meant evil against me but God turned it into a good thing and bring you to what you are today to keep you alive.``
Joseph lived in his father's house with his sons Ephraim and Manasseh and their children.

When Joseph became old he finally said to his brothers. "God will visit you after my death and bring you out of Egypt so they won't have to strive.``

Joseph was an old man when he died and was buried in Egypt before there was a massive Exodus and both he and his father were dead

----

The Miss International Heaven Beauty Pageant, in competition with Earth and World Pageants, began in Toronto in 2014.

The Pageant is eligible for global beauties between ages thirty and eighteen.

The winner becomes Saint Peters assistant gate keeper at 12 Pearly Gates.

On different dates.

If admitted to heaven, the winner will see the prettiest sight one has ever seen.

--

The 3 global finalists were from Canada, Ethiopia and Philippines.

Canada's candidate was lovely Yvonne Cocteau, and was asked a question by Saint Brother Andrea who at one time lived in Montreal and when posing his question was wearing jeans.

The question was: "When you die what have you done or are doing now in order to deserve entry to heaven? Her reply was: "I spoke about God on school and mall tours and the global environment change that is taking place,"
Miss Cocteau answered her question with grace.
Even after she had said, "I hope the Maple Leafs with the Stanley Cup by all means.
--

The Ethiopian candidate was pretty Azusa Adawa,
And was asked the same question by Saint Abraham who at one time lived in Addis Ababa.
Her reply was: I'm helping the poor and homeless even when its night at eleven.
In Addis Ababa and heaven.
And pray that an Ethiopian wins the 100 meter dash during the next summer Olympics.
His family name is Birwa.

--

The Filipino candidate was beautiful Pasita Cruz.
And was asked the same question by Saint Lorenzo Ruiz.
Pasita's reply was: "Since I'm a Muslim I have read the Koran and prayed to Allah that the Mindanao part of the Philippines becomes a separated Muslim State, since I was eleven. Each day I also pray that the UN asks the Filipino government to get rid of its political corruption within 2 years so that I can enter heaven.
And in that time, to act fast and not snooze."

What is a Canadian invention?
That's a good question.
A Canadian has invented the Key frame animation.
Multi-Dynamic Teqnique – IMax Movie System – the Track ball for DATAR computer information.
For any nation.

--

In Food and Agriculture, what did Canadians invent?
Canadians invented Poutine – Nanaimo bar – Canola made from rape seed – Marquis wheat – Macintosh red apple – Yukon Gold Potato.
Pablum – Ginger Ale – the Butter Tart – Instant mashed potato which one can eat with a Tomato.
This is some food Canada to the world has sent.
--
What Canadian invention is there in Communication?
Graham Bell invented the first telephone. A Canadian invented the Walkie-Talkie – Cesium Beam atomic clock – the Brunton compass – Amplitude Modulation - the BlackBerry by which one can contact Don Cherry without frustration.
Also, radio telephony – the Fathometer – Computerized Braille – Standard time – the Pager – 56k modem to be used in any situation.
Without complication or frustration.
--

Did Canadians invent anything in Transportation and Mobility?
They certainly did. The first wheelchair accessible to a bus – Separate baggage check – the Hydrofoil boat – first jetliner to fly in America – Overhead power connection for electric street cars – the Canadarm – snowmobile – Crash position indicator for stability.
The Parcelo (partial clover leaf interchange) - Unimotorcycle.
JACO, a robotic arm for the wheelchair – electric heater – prosthetic hand – Electric car heater and the Bixi bicycle.
Which offers flexibility.
--

Are there Climate and Defence inventions by a Canadian?
There are: the Snow blower – Steam powered fog horn –
Which can be used on the Mediterranean?
Rotary snowplows for railroads – the first widely used as mask – the G-suit – Sonar – ASDC – CADPAT, the first "digital" camouflage system, which can e used even if one is a vegetarian.
An Episcopalian Iranian or an Australian.

Is there a Canadian who invented something in Entertainment or Sport?
You bet: Instant replay – Trivia Pursuit – Five pin bowling - Lacrosse – Basketball and Hockey.
For the world to be lucky.
When it comes to science and medicine, Doctor Frederick Banting co-invented Medicinal Insulin – First electric microscope – A process to extract Bromide – A process for Producing Calcium Carbide for Acetylene which can be used at a seaport.

--

What has a Canadian invented to help domestic life – Have you got a list?
I do: Pablum – Nanaimo tart – Plexi glass - Easy Off – the Garbage bag – without a mist.
The Modern Wonderbra.
That is popular in Moose Jaw.
Also: Cardiac pacemaker – Alkaline Battery – Caulking gun – Electric oven
Paint roller – Robertson screw – Rotary vane pump – Automatic lubricating cup.
I'm sure there are more inventions on the list and I'm sorry if they have been missed.

Mary Jane keeps hopping.
Waiting for deals during the annual **Black Friday** shopping.
During November of the year.
Which is near.
Retail prices will be dropping.
Practice makes perfect.
There's no reason to object.
If you want to learn how to skateboard.
And win a reward.
What you will learn, you will not regret.
--
Eileen.
Is a pretty teen.
The prettiest I have ever seen.
Who goes out trick and treating.
During Halloween with her friend Dean.
--
Clara Stewart.
Was bright and she knew it.
While baking a birthday cake.
She had made a mistake
And said, Ah, screw it."
--

While living in Moose Jaw.
Irene left her ma and pa.
To live common-law.
Which lead her father say, "Hurrah!"
It was the most dysfunctional family I ever saw.
--
Dominic Fare
Invented a sandwich called a donair
Which now is enjoyed everywhere
In fast food restaurants and if you take care
At the summer or winter fair
--
Don Brown
Lives in a small New Brunswick town
One day while going fishing and fell down
That caused him to frown
As he had lost his dental tooth crown
--
My love for you
Has always been true
Even when I'm blue
Or suffering the flu.
I know your games. I have played the too
--

There are hawks flying over
Our field of sweet clover.
The hawks are trying to find small birds with laughter
But not after
They are picked up, eaten and their life is over.

--

By our gate
I ask you to wait
When I return from Pakistan
And Afghanistan
And then you will become my ever loving mate

--

Now I must depart to fight and stop ISIS in Iraq, Syria
and Libya
Where Islamic State extremists are causing a humanitarian tragedy.
by beheading , setting on fire, Christians, hostages, women and children whenever the terrorist are ready
And preparing to seize Iran's nuclear secrets and you friend Sylvia

--

What's more dear Alicia, you are what I prayed for
And what's more
I'd like to see you in the café
Across the way
From the Superstore
--
My name is Joe.
A dog follows me everywhere I go.
Even if the weather is 20 below
And I walk slow.
On my way to see a puppet show.
--
Sue Bickle.
Gave me a nickel.
To buy her a dill pickle.
This sounded kind of fickle.
So she also gave me a tickle.
--
Agnes Possibility.
At work is a liability.
She became silly.
As soon as she fell in love with Willy.
From Piccadilly.
--

Molly Berry had no clue
What she was going through
First she was swimming in a pool
That was cool
At a time she was suffering from the flu too
--
Hold me close to your heart
And make sure you don't fart
If you do, it will tear out relationship apart
That shouldn't have had a start.
And both of at the time thought we were smart
--
I did not marry you because you have curly hair and beautiful chin
And using all sort of creams on your skin
I married you
Because you are you
And can play the violin
--
A can of green beans.
Was given to the marines.
That had little means
While taking their vaccines
 So they wore blue jeans.
--

Sarah Hughes.
Wore a pair of high heel shoes.
Following a drink of booze.
She fell down and had a bruise
That is the sad news.

--

There is reason.
Why I feel different each season.
It might be treason
But as the seasons change I have poor vision.
Without any kind of reason.

--

Jane lives in Tonasket.
And keeps her lunch in a basket.
While playing broomball.
Basketball,
Or making a funeral casket.

--

Mary was a prolific dancer.
Who had a soul of a panther.
She died after a battle with breast cancer,
Although there was no anger.
Why cancer? Friends wanted an answer.

--

Lorraine.
Moved to Edmonton from Ukraine.
Every day that it would rain.
She had to use an umbrella and a cane.
Because of her arthritis pain.
Now and again.
--
On the internet there is a dating scam.
Example: Jane and Sam.
Jane registers on line for a possible romantic relationship.
And Dam acknowledges he wants companionship.
Sam and Jane communicate by email and over time Jane claims she needs financial assistance. Sam complies and soon realizes he has been duped, while Jane pockets the money and moves on to find another victim like Sam.
--

So you thought publishing your dream book came true.
And you didn't know the Self-Book Publisher is deceiving you.
It charges a high price for publishing your book but sales are few.
Self-book publishing isn't a route to follow if an author is new.
And the respect due to you.
--
Avoid Work-At-Home scams as there are many.
First one has to buy software for more than a penny.
Then with the help of a guru, click on the internet and your millions start rolling in.
One doesn't do anything but literally watch your bank account rise where ever you are or have been.
For peace of mind one should be aware of the fraudulent WAH scam. Especially if one is a Granny.
--

In Montreal Etienne Bateau had a friend named Dick.
A UFO skeptic.
"The alien you see above", he says. "Is a shadow of the moon.
Or a drifting balloon."
Have your pick.

--

A UFO landed in North Dakota.
But the breaks didn't work one iota.
It didn't take long.
To decide what was wrong.
Seems the space ship was made by Toyota.

--

After having been to Planet Mars.
I came home with several scars.
And went through several cars.
Lost two guitars.
Worse of all, I landed behind bars.

--

It's a quarter past three.
My friends are looking for me.
While my parents are away.
I'm in the bathroom most of the day.
Because I'm afraid to have a sting by the killer bee.

--

Jack says, "Ouija Boards aren't a game with numbers selected by hand".
Nellie says, "Scary isn't it? Ouija Boards uncover mysteries of the land.
Frank says, "I strongly believe in the power Ouija Boards hold".
Elizabeth says, "And the spiritual mysteries they can unfold."
Religious groups however, say, "Seancing with spirits is a hoax and thus Ouija Boards should be banned."

--

Each October the Alberta town of Smoky Lake holds a Big Pumpkin Contest.
Entries come from provinces in the West.
Pumpkins weighing about 1500 pounds are considered the best.
Contest losers may feel depressed.
They however, do not protest and have confessed that the chairman weighing the pumpkins has a reputation of being honest.

--

In United States, the New Hampshire
Pumpkin Festival.
Must have been visited by the devil.
Mayhem took place caused by booze.
As crowds were throwing everything things at each other, including their shoes.
There were injuries and arrests. To be honest the festival did not go well.
--

For a Heritage Food Festival in Edmonton present was a cook from Africa's Cameroon.
Unfortunately Phil Yang had his date mixed up and arrived a bit too soon.
When the correct time did arrive Phil cooked a cuisine of cassava, cocoyam, plantain, rice and yams.
Along with various jams.
And then went to sleep until noon.
--

There was a young Marshall, Saskatchewan a man named Stu.
Who watched his wife Sandy, making stew.
But on that day there was a mistake.
In the stove that she did bake.
Ann's cooking time needed a review.
--

In the Saskatchewan village of Cut Knife,
Mother Andrea Smitten one day said:
"I'm so happy our teenage son Brad isn't bad.
He helps his father, mother and brother.
Like no other.
And doesn't feel helping others is a dread.
--
A Canadian invented the game of basketball.
Where to succeed a player must be tall.
A Canadian also invented the game of hockey.
Where the players should be sturdy and stocky.
The best Canadian sport invention I enjoy the most is broomball.
--
There's a young Stettler, Alberta hockey player named Foley.
A terrific goalie.
His must be holy.
Because whenever there is a slaps Shot heading for his face, he
Falls to his knees and yells, "Hallelujah! Am I ever glad that before the game I had a dish of ravioli.
What a save! Holy. Moly!"
--

My basketball sneakers can make me fly.
While in grade five I could jump high.
I wasn't the best player on the team.
But it was my dream.
With these shoes I swear I could touch the sky.
--
In the Saskatchewan town of Biggar, lives Emmy Case, an upcoming tennis star.
Who many thought would go far.
But one day on the tennis court she slipped and fell down.
And had no chance to win a crown.
Poor Emmy did not go far.
--
At the Calgary Stampede a cowboy named Bert
Met a young lady with a short skirt.
His face turned red.
As he spluttered and said:
You are lovely, You are shapely and a flirt."
--

Hennessey is a Toronto jockey that stood at 4 foot 6.
And knew all the horse racing tricks.
At one time was asked, "Was your horse ever drugged?"
He shrugged.
And then said, "Only once for kicks."
--
Joe Pappa was a boxing fighter.
Who one day in September, boxed Bert Terwiliger.
That was ten pounds lighter
But considerably smarter.
And brighter.
--
In Trail, B. C, Don Seier.
Was a weekly skier.
One day he fell on the Red Mountain top.
And did not stop.
To say hello to friend, Dan Frier.
--
The Saint Catherine's, Ontario, old timer's line up for a 3 mile run.
A fundraiser for the Food Bank and have fun.
They are on their toes.
As excitement goes.
But 5 collapse at the sound of the starter gun,

In Hamilton, there was a young swimmer named Ivor
Who was also a diver.
He dived with a twist.
One day the deep water he missed.
And was lucky to be a survivor.
--
This October 3, 2014 when Eid is a Muslim religious feast of ending the fast.
Following Ramadam during the ninth month of the year that has just past.
At the same time Jewish people celebrate Yon Kippur.
It's a holy day of fasting, atonement and redemption for the rich and the poor.
While Christians too celebrate traditions but they don't long last.
--
It's tense in Hong Kong.
No time to play ping pong.
Tension persists.
As the Beijing Communist government resists.
To have a free election. Beijing says one would be wrong
--

In the Saskatchewan village of Delisle, a single parent mother named Alicia Kuppy.
Wants a 40-month maternity leave because she owns a two month puppy.
Her employer denied the request and said.
"To bad.
I suggest you see a psychiatrist because to me you seem to be a bit nutty."
--
Canada has a national animal, the maple leaf and an anthem.
But no national dance that we can fathom.
So the Canada Arts Council approved a dance about Canadian patriotism.
To show our French and English bilingualism and nationalism.
And our Inner Sanctum.
--
At one time Edmonton's slogan was the City of Champions and Gateway to the North.
And in 2015 it's going forth.
to change the symbol to read: Official City Portal to the Universe.
Portal means entrance and a large purse.
With the oil boom the city hopes to blossom forth.

While traveling in a British Columbia forest near Nelson, Stan Proudfoot ran into the mysterious Sasquatch better known as the hominid-like creature Bigfoot.
Stan blew his car horn toot, toot, and toot.
As the car came closer he noticed Bigfoot was covered with soot and was barefoot.
Until Bigfoot disappeared Stan had to stay put.

--

In 2013 the Boston Red Sox produced a joyful elate.
When they won the World Series number eight.
MVP was slugger David Ortiz.
His home runs were the keys.
In ending 95 years of a home wait.

--

In Vancouver, during White Caps soccer game there was an import striker from Clyde.
Who hated his breakfast eggs boiled or fried.
When asked, "Why?"
"It's just because I.
Am a poacher by trade." he replied.

--

In Alberta's Cold Lake there's an angler named Tony.
His friends thought he was full of baloney.
He went to Cold Lake West.
Where fished with the best.
Pictures prove that he's no phoney.
--
Ken Fischer.
Is a trout fisher.
He fishes in Moose Lake,
And also Cold lake,
In all kinds of weather and pressure.
--
Near Calgary's Bow River there's a biker named Reed.
Who bypassed a hiker's need.
When offered some franks.
He said, "No thanks.
As I already have what I need."
--

While cycling uphill near Jasper we finally got it made.
It was a hot summer with plenty of shade.
From home it is far.
So I asked by partner "Can you guess where we are?"
I don't care." he replied.
His name is Jason Jade.
--
Who, who, who!
Dearest Lulu.
Where are you?
"I'm on the golfing with few.
Wishing you were with me too."
--
Alberta/B. C. Skiing Resorts are seeking a high-tech edge.
A dazzling new move to improve their pledge.
To make a lift chip REID software that uses a wireless electric magnate.
To improve ticket sales which at present are stagnate.
This includes a skiing resort in Rossland,
 B. C. which is named Red.
--

It would have nice to have a snooze.
But during the month of June there is no time to lose.
After yesterday's rain.
Sun and wind came again.
Perfect weather for drying my shoes.
--
When your Thanksgiving Day is misty and murky.
You are inside the house happy and perky.
There are people to great.
Pumpkin pie and lots of goodies to eat.
And please say a prayer for the turkey.
--
This Christmas I'm writing to you.
Our friendship to renew.
May the season be glad.
The best that you ever had.
And all your dreams come true.
--

World News Report
In Africa more than 10.000 die from EBOLA.
Including Liberia
Eve Morales re-elected for the third time as president of Bolivia
World economy plummets – Oil now under $50 a barrel.
World economists ask, "What the hell?"
The West air strikes ISIS terrorists in Iraq and Syria.
--
 In New Glasgow, Nova Scotia, there was an odious brute.
Who made love in his Sunday-best suit.
The result, as you you'd guess.
Was a suit in a mess.
And a chafed maiden to boot.
--
A pretty maiden from France.
Decided she'd take a chance.
She'd let herself go,
For an hour or so.
And now all her sisters are aunts.
--

A man in Vancouver,
Was left by his lover.
He pulled his hair,
In shear despair.
Forgetting a wig was his only cover.
--
Please be my valentine.
And then my life will be fine.
No, don't shake your head.
Let's just jump into bed,
And we'll finish that bottle of wine.
--
You are my favorite valentine.
That makes me shine.
And a friend.
That is why I want to send
A message to be my life-time valentine.
--
In Edmonton at one time there was a hotel named York.
Who as a child, the owner was brought into Canada by a stork.
As an adult he had daughter,
Hired a tutor who taught her,
How to properly eat using a fork.
--

Latest World News Report --
In New Brunswick, for shooting three cops, Dustin Borbeau sentenced to life imprisonment.
San Francisco Giants wins baseball World Series with magnificent pitching and little temperament.
Mr. Hockey, Gordie Howe, .is in serious health condition.
With Ukraine, Russia's Vladimir Putin is still fishing,
More than 5000 in 8 African countries die from EBOLA, a World disappointment.
--
Canadian investors are now saying "Doom, Doom!
There's plenty of oil gloom.
If one is to invest on the moon.
Or In Rangoon.
Where, what, when and with whom?"
--

Eastern Canada currently imports 86 percent of its oil from foreign sources.
From countries that do not share our values and resources.
So let Canada stand up for energy independence, a safer world and stronger.
And wait no longer.
In time to have a pipeline to the east, which the Canadian government endorses.
--
For a 20 Alberta Oil Sands group.
Cook Boris with a swoop.
Made a vegetable soup.
When eaten, most of the troop.
Had to go and poop.
--
The Alberta Oil Sands contractor had a cook.
Who mistook a soup recipe from a foreign cook book.
The soup turned out to be gobbllegook.
As the employees while eating shook and shook.
As the correct recipe the cook forgot to look.
--

The latest world news headlines –
Taliban kill 132 children in a school in Pakistan.
Another earthquake in Japan.
An Iranian gunman, Haron Monis, holds 16 hostages in an Australian café.
Russian economy collapses as the ruble drops in value today.
Atomic Entergy talks continue between the West and Iran.
--
U. S. president Obama ends 50 year standoff with Cuba.
Now Obama can play the tuba.
And be a protector of merchants like the Budha
And learn how to swim using a scuba
And dance the juba.
--
If I were a fly, I would take my place.
In the House of Commons where haste makes waste.
I'd buzz to the Speakers ear.
Because it has become clear.
The voice of the Canadian public has been misplaced.
--

Yesterday I saw the biblical epic movie **Exodus** which cost 80-million dollars to make.

Because of its historical, religious errors t would be better if money spent was on. 'How Aunt Jemima makes a pancake'.

Not once does the movie mention Moses in the Hebrew drive out of Egypt.

The movie tries to use the Ten Commandments manuscript.

But it failed and for a movie goer like me. It's hard to take.

--

Elizabeth was a Toronto dame.
Who knew no shame.
She weighed more than 200 pounds.
And made all sort of strange sounds.
In her baboon-like frame.

--

Gina was a Swiss supermodel.
Who taught people how to yodel.
She yodeled on a street.
In her bare feet.
To tunes by German composer George Handel. (1685-1759)

--

Do not forget that the oil boom-doom rhymes.
In these trouble times.
And oil tycoons chatter.
What is the matter?
In Alberta and the Maritimes.

--

Before you start.
Make certain you have a strong heart.
And are smart.
While checking your landscape art.
That is falling apart.

--

It's a sad tale.
That ice has covered Huron Lake.
And now no one can sail.
Male or Female.
Because it's beginning to hail.

--

In the Yukon it's snowing and very cold.
Affecting people that are old.
So cold, a snow shovel one cannot hold.
And we are told.
Not to pan for gold.

--

In my heart and head.
I wanted a slice of bread.
Denied, my face turned red.
So I said:
O. K. "I'm going ahead to my bed."
--
In a bright light.
During a stormy night.
I had a terrific fright
Wondering if ever I might
Fly a kite.
--
I had a spade.
Wondering if I could make a trade.
So I prayed.
When out comes a maid.
Following a Home Hardware raid.
--
To a passing cloud.
I was proud.
Stopped and bowed.
In front of a large crowd.
That was extremely loud.
--

Cameron cried.
When he lost his beautiful bride.
Her search was wide.
Where she might hide.
She was found several hours later, hugging a security guide.
--
The village minstrels sing.
On a street about everything.
Even if they have no wing/
And an ants bite sting.
To the minstrels, such a hazards did not mean a thing.
--
The way Ted was raised.
By his friends he was praised.
During holidays.
Or dining in cafes.
He was acknowledged with many Hoorays!
--
I'm amazed.
By many ways.
To enjoy holidays.
And after your trip the memory stays.
When one is organized and not dazed.
--

Clara cannot tell a lie.
And the reason is why.
There is no denying.
That she is lying.
Because she's expected to die.
--
I'm amazed at the Rocky Mountains.
And the nearby fountains.
I'm amazed at its green forest.
Wild animals and the florist.
Next to the dolphins.
--
I was sitting in a restaurant enjoying my favourite meal.
When a stranger sat next to me and my wallet he did steal.
As I was watching a pretty girl go by.
And she began to cry.
After she had lost a high heal.
--
What's the best thing since sliced bread?
Iraq's Saddam Hussein has been dead.
Warren Buffet has become a billionaire.
And Microsoft's Bill Gates doesn't care.
To charities their wealth they spread.
--

Joyful of mind.
And being kind.
You'll not be in a mess.
But success.
Of every kind.
--
At my elderly age.
It's time to turn a page.
Go back stage.
Get rid of my rage.
And try to earn a better wage.
--
Chunky Charlie.
Enjoyed soup with barley.
Made by Farley.
Became snarly.
And then went on a safari.
--
Hey Joe! How was your holiday?
Did you get more pay?
No need to belabour the point.
Are still working for the same joint?
If you are, come my way.
--

You spent a lot of time to find me a special gift.
That would give my life a lift.
On my special day.
As you often say.
"I want to be kissed and not missed."
--
With no hair out of place.
And no whisker on his face
Jake entered a race.
Trying to keep pace.
With his mother-in-law, Grace
--
I heard Niagara Falls roar.
At the Rocky Mountain highway I swore.
I have been to the Grand Canyon.
And saw a statue of Paul Bunyan.
The Swiss Alps and the Caribbean seashore.
--
There is one thing you should know.
In Canada there is lot of snow.
Winter temperature reaches up to 40 below.
Climate change is slow.
This happened a year ago.
--

In Canada we pray for rain during summer.
And nearly freeze to death during winter.
In summer one can easily find a lover.
In winter one is a bit dumber.
Than their father and mother.

--

My pet dog, Little Joe.
Is sweet wherever we go.
That is why I use a mace.
He doesn't lick my face.
And my belly button below.

--

My friend Andy.
Loves his candy.
And felt dandy.
Until I gave him a brandy.
Then he wasn't handy.

--

Greta.
Can sing an operetta.
Although she has sore knees.
But, oh boy, can she tease.
More than poet, Andrieta.

--

There's a Vancouver man named Earl
Who gives life a whirl.
He has his own jet.
And seldom does he get wet.
With his piolet an ex Bunny Girl.
--
Rose.
Had the finest clothes.
But she was unreasonable
As it was unseasonable.
And she nearly froze.
--
I recently went to a grocery store.
Where there were food items galore.
There were vegetables and meat.
And items that are sweet.
And some that made my eyes sore.
--
Wendy Deere
Has wax in her ear
Water drips from her nose
Has corn on toes.
And once in a while loves to have a drink of beer.
--

The problem with Pastor Ed.
Is he keeps rising from the dead.
Heaven, Purgatory and Hell.
All things might be well.
"But I rather be in church." he said.

--

We holiday each month of June.
A time when there is a full moon.
We eat what we please.
Including hamburgers with cheese.
Not having to use a fork, knife or a spoon

--

Bring me bread and bring me wine.
And we will dine.
While feeling fine.
During sunshine.
And no whine.

--

The Canadian loonie is lowest in six years.
And there are fears.
As it dropped 80-cents U. S. and further will slide.
Canadian pride will hide.
From coast to coast, to coast, to coast in order not to shed tears.

--

In Canada federal prisons to eliminate fresh milk.
And switch to powdered milk.
The Canadian government is expected to save 3.1 M a year.
While the taste will not be the same, prisoners frown and fear.
No matter what their ilk.
--
An oil construction worker near Fort McMurray called Nick.
Did an unusual trick.
He would sit on a stool and jiggle his hammer and wrench tool.
That is cool.
And then he would say: "The trick, hammer or wrench. Have your pick."
--
Flu deaths surge in Alberta this season.
And there is good reason.
Vaccines seem to provide little or no protection.
And there is need for a correction.
Otherwise it could be a case of treason.
--

There was an oil worker in Drayton Valley.
Who with his wife Sally.
Discussing the low price of oil and the Canadian dollar value dropping.
When they didn't agree and after stopping.
They went to the Whitewood Restaurant for breakfast and a cup of tea.

--

In Mission B. C. I met a monk who could inspire.
Espousing his spiritual fire,.
As soon as I found.
He was profound.
I could also call him a friar.

--

In Esterhazy, Saskatchewan, Jan Pulaski had a habit.
Each day to fee a stray rabbit.
When it ate a carrot.
He then fed a ferret.
And then his own parrot.

--

In Whistler B. C a skiing lady named Katie.
A lovely blue eye. Red haired lady.
Came to ski from Hawaii.
And said, "Howdee."
She was a bit weighty

There once a man named Seville.
Who lived in the town of Vegreville.
On Highway 36 his car broke down.
Two miles from the town.
So he towed his car to Bonnyville.
--
An atheist was fishing in Okanagan Lake.
And must have made a mistake.
When the monster Ogopogo tossed him and boat into the air.
Although he did care.
All he could do is shake and shake.
--
Latest World headline Report;--
In Paris 1700 people killed by Islamic terrorists.
The EBOLO epidemic in West Africa still exists.
Target is closing its 133 Canadian stores..
Deadly Boko Harem attacks in Nigeria soars.
Air Asian plane with 162 passengers found in Java Sea, One of the 3
recent plane crash incidents,
--

Shlumberger is one of the world's largest oilfield companies.
Employing approximately 126,000 people in 85 countries.
Founded in 1926 by French bothers Conrad and Marcel Shlumberger.
The giant companies operated full-time from January to December.
An in January, 2015 slashed 900 jobs, One of several surprises.
--
As of late.
Things are going great.
I published a book.
How to catch fish without using a hook.
While accompanied with Charlotte, my mate.
--
Pope Francis is in the Philippines. (January 2015)
For several reasons.
To comfort the 2013 Tahloban typhoon survivors.
And pray for the poor children who have desires.
To improve their life by being able to go to school.
In a new pair of jeans.

Prominent Italian Canadians --
Michael Buble, Jason Spezza, Phil Esposito
Marty Turko, Gino Vanelli, Guy Lombardo.
Luis Pasaglia, Fernando Pisani, Hank Biasuti
Ray Ferraro, Dino Cicarelli, Arturo Gatti
Enrico Colantonia, Sandro Grande, Dino Bravo
--
Prominent Ukrainian Canadians --
Frank Basaraba, Eugene Melnyk
Chantel Kreviazuk, Ed Stelmnach
Ray Hnatyshyn, Wall Stanowski
 Alexander Dubas, Kelly Hrudy Peter Podrosky
Roberta Bodnar, Alec Trebek
--
Prominent Filipino Canadians --
Prudensio Perez, Alex Pagulayan, Ernesto Baldovino
Conrad Santos, Nini Tan, Loeonila Mateo.
Shay Mitchell, Emilio Gonsalem, Yvonne Patel
Liza Doig, Felix Jochin, Gerry Domingo, Teofista Actuel
John Tonelli, Milda Greshner, Steve Nilo
--

Prominent Polish Canadians –
Alexandra Wozniak, Stanley Remesz, Peter Gzowski
Benjamin Kowaoewicz, Andrew Mynarski
Turk Broda. Allan Wachowitch, Henry Wojecicki
Stefan Sznuk, Liza Ray, Devon Sawa, Jan Swederski
John Tavares, Geddy Lee, Isaac Hellmuth, Wayne Gretzky
--
Prominent German Canadians –
John Diefenbaker, Justin Bieber, Randy Bachman, Scott and Rob Niedermayer
Ralph Klein, Candy Classen, k. d. lang.
Howie Morenz, Valerie Poxleitner
Jack Layton, Milt Schmidt, Bobby Bauer, Jonathan Wagner, Garry Doer
Almuth Lukenhaus, Volcaire Ries, Karl Friesen, Albert Greshner, Matt Brouwer
Frank Stronach, John Vernon, Agustus Vogt, Eberhard Zeidler.
--

Jewish Canadian writers –
Ted Allan, Leonard Cohan, Fritz Heichelheim
Nordecai Richler, Stephen Lewis, Elyse Goldstein
Ezra Lavant, Mel Hurtig, Michael Neumann
Goldie Morganthaler, Major Gross, Peter, C Newman
Saul Below. Leonard Pickoff, A. M. Klein
--
Arab Canadians –
Kevin O'Leary, Christina Maria, Reema Abdo, David Azzi
Paul Anka, Lorraine Michael, Joe Hadad, Nazem Kadri
Joe Giz, Mohammed Boudjenane. Andy Kim
Kamal Halabi, Omar Najjar, Rene Angelilm Albert Rahaiem.
Naria Mourani, Emil Francis, Karl Wolf, Mamdouh Shoukari
--

Current Canadian pop singers –
Neil Young, Diana Krall, Anne Murray,
Gordon Lightfoot, Tom Cochrane,
Leonard Cohan, Bryan Adams, Henry Burr,
Randy Bachman
Joni Mitchel, Paul Anka, Michael Buble,
Alanis Morissette
Paul Brandt, Jann Arden, Avril Lavign, Aron Pritchett
Ian Tyson. Celine Dione, k. d. lang, Nelly
Fortada, Sarah McLachlan who is always in a hurry.
--
Halfway through my career.
When I was a cashier.
 Jason Bo was near.
When I enjoyed my first beer.
1997 was the year.
--
At last spring is here and in Vancouver cherry tree blossoms are budding.
Jack and Jane are hugging
Now that it's a bit warmer.
On the Robson corner.
And not afraid to receive a drubbing.
--

Nobody knows.
How the future goes.
If my mother crochets or sews.
My brother Charlie, chases crows
At a time when it snows.
--
It's a long way to Ontario's city of Cornwall.
To see its new shopping mall.
Jack is tall.
His wife Kate is small.
Before entering the mall they stumble and have a fall.
--
A dairy farmer in Langley, B. C. by the name of Carl Howe.
Purchased another milking cow.
That had to be milked right now.
After milking her Carl made a bow.
And excitedly said, "What wonderful milk to drink? Wow!"
--

The year 2015 is here and so are 3 Friday's
the 13th which to some cause fear.
It's an unlucky day in Western superstition far
away and near,
The superstition may have arisen because of a
double whammy of Jesus' Last Supper and
Crucifixion took place. And Eve offered
Adam the forbidden fruit on Friday the 13th.
And not on the 14th or 15th.
Fear of the number 13 is called
paraskevidekaphobia. Oh what a word!. I'm
sorry my dear.
--
In numerology, the number 12 is considered
the number of completeness. As reflected in
the 12 months of the year.
With no fear.
12 hours on the clock day, 12 deities of
Olympus, 12 tribes of Israel,12 apostles of
Jesus, the 12 successors of Muhammad in
Shia Islam, 12 signs of the Zodiac, 12 years of
the Chinese Buddhist cycle.
As approved by Saint Michael.
In contrast the number 13 is considered
irregular , transgressing this completeness.
And not shedding a tear because everything is
oh so clear.

In Oromotco, New Brunswick, Sarah and Hugh.
Were discussing their Dream De Je Vous.
To which to them the dream was new.
And they didn't know what to do.
For fear their dreams were true.
--
In the Saskatchewan town of Kindersley there is a woodpecker.
Who has been named Necktor.
He continual pecks and pecks damaging a tree in order to make a nest.
And the rest:
Poor birdie woodpecker is a tree wrecker.
--
One day discontent Sam roared: "I don't' give a damn.
About what happens in Viet Nam.
I am who I am.
This isn't a scam.
To understand my feeling. See me quickly as you can. Otherwise I'll have to scram!"
--

World News headlines --
Canadian supreme court approves with a doctors help one can commit a death suicide.
In United States and Canada there's a measles outbreak that is country wide.
It's Goodbye ensign, Welcome maple leaf flag, on your 50th birthday.
Russia and Ukraine sign a peace treaty but more trouble not far away.
ISIS burns a captured Jordanian piolet to death and says it's not a lie.
--
At a New York art museum named Cloisters.
I had a meal of clams, mussels, shrimp, crabs, scallops and oysters.
Which was expensive to cost.
Even during a day of frost.
And one is in a state of cloister's.
--
Andy was lonely.
While eating a sandwich with baloney.
Next day he was having a pizza.
And met pretty Rita.
For Andy, the one and only.
--

We must agree.
That our true love will be.
Everlasting and strong.
Even when things go wrong.
Between you and me.
--
This is the last time.
 I'm going to whine
If you don't give me a kiss
When we miss
Seeing Michael Buble before there is another Edmonton crime.
--
Goodbye moon.
Goodbye smartphone.
Goodbye baboon.
And the friendly racoon.
Hope to see you soon.
--
In Canada there's a revolution.
To find a solution.
To drive an electric car.
With a battery one can drive far.
If need be with a government contribution.
--

Bulletin! An Edmonton scientist by the name
of Jason Bell.
Has just invented a car that runs by a fuel cell.
The software is free.
And between you and me,
The oil sands producers near Fort McMurray.
I'm sorry to say, aren't doing well.
--
While putting this limerick book together,
I was under the weather.
And thanks to my wife Fe.
She took care of me throughout night and day.
During all kinds of weather.
--

Made in the USA
Charleston, SC
13 December 2015